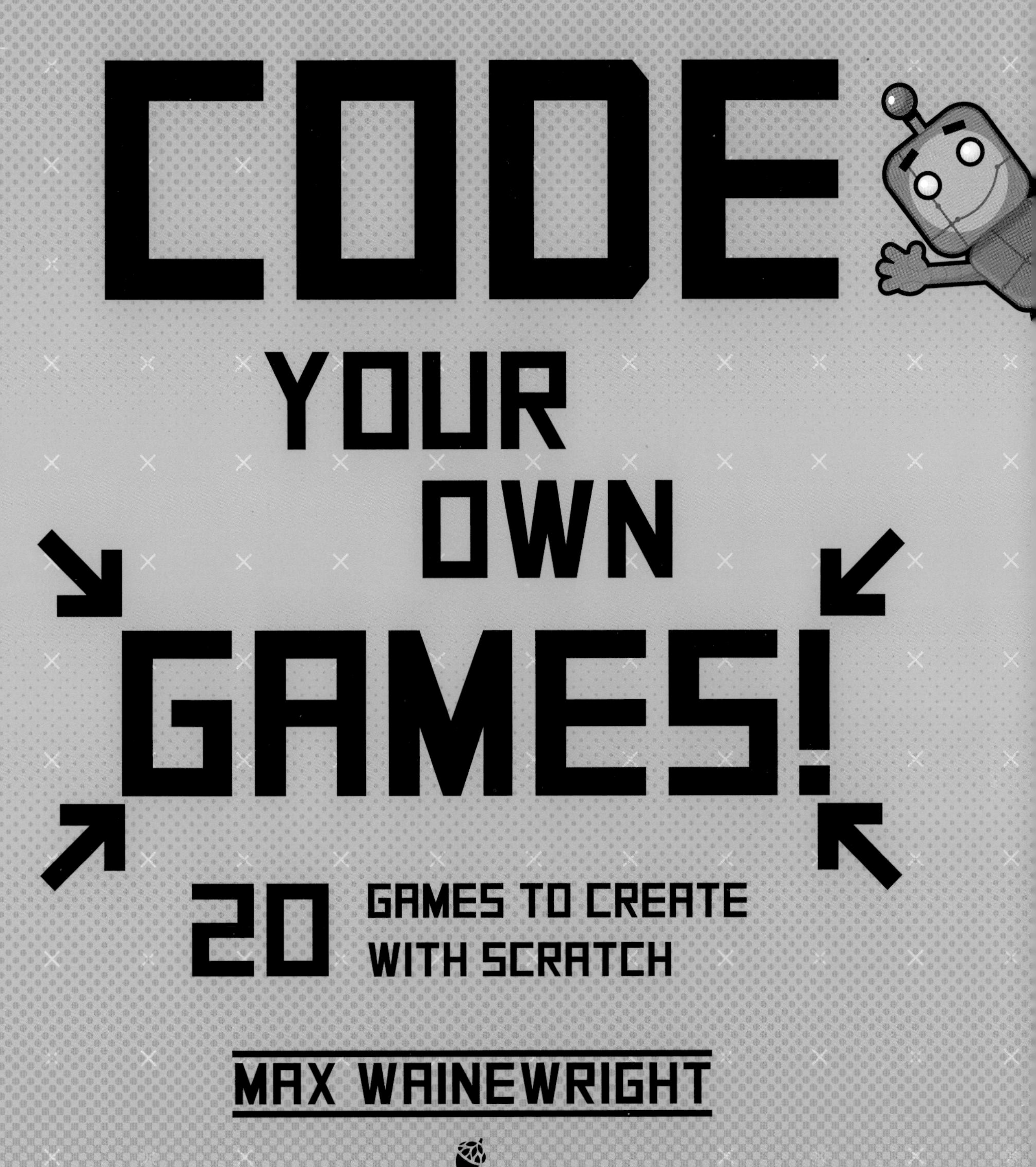

CODE YOUR OWN GAMES!

20 GAMES TO CREATE WITH SCRATCH

MAX WAINEWRIGHT

STERLING CHILDREN'S BOOKS
New York

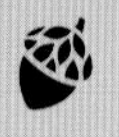

STERLING CHILDREN'S BOOKS
New York

An Imprint of Sterling Publishing Co., Inc.
1166 Avenue of the Americas
New York, NY 10036

STERLING CHILDREN'S BOOKS and the distinctive
Sterling Children's Books logo are registered trademarks of Sterling Publishing Co., Inc.

First Sterling edition published in 2017.

ISBN 978-1-4549-2331-2

Distributed in Canada by Sterling Publishing
Canadian Manda Group, 664 Annette Street, Toronto, Ontario, Canada, M6S 2C8

For information about custom editions, special sales, and premium and corporate purchases, please contact Sterling Special Sales at 800-805-5489 or specialsales@sterlingpublishing.com.

Manufactured in China

Lot #:
4 6 8 10 9 7 5
03/18

www.sterlingpublishing.com

Scratch is developed by the Lifelong Kindergarten Group at MIT Media Lab.
See **http://scratch.mit.edu**

Information on resources

You can use Scratch on a PC or Mac by opening your web browser and going to: **http://scratch.mit.edu**
Then click **"Try it out."**

There is a very similar website called "Snap," which also works on iPads. It is available here:
http://snap.berkeley.edu/run

If you want to run Scratch without using the web, you can download it here:
http://scratch.mit.edu/scratch2download/

Internet safety

Children should be supervised when using the internet, particularly when using an unfamiliar website for the first time. The publishers and author cannot be held responsible for the content of the websites referred to in this book.

CONTENTS

WHAT MAKES A GOOD GAME?

Hello!

This book will show you how to code twenty awesome games using Scratch. You won't just learn how to build the games, you'll also get to have fun playing them! By the time you've tried out these games, you will have mastered the coding skills to design and build your *own* games. But first, what do you think makes a good game?

MOVEMENT, SPEED, AND OBSTACLES?

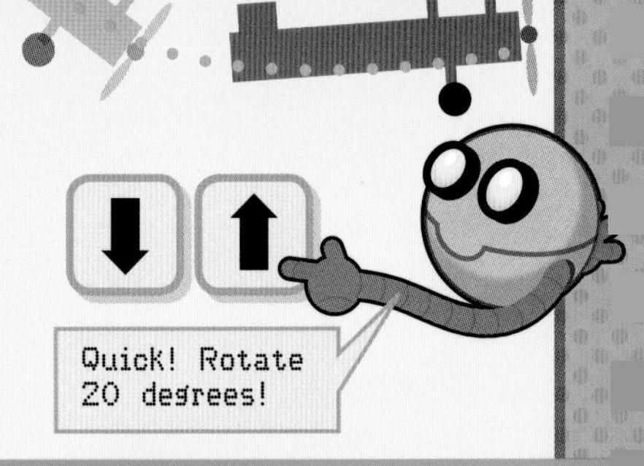

Quick! Rotate 20 degrees!

A good game tests your skills to the max. How fast can you drive the race car? How high can you fly the helicopter?

In this book, you'll learn to create code so you can use the keyboard or mouse to control the movement of cars, planes, and characters. You'll also learn to use coding loops, so movements happen again and again—and your race car will keep racing!

Most games have obstacles to overcome. Perhaps your snake has to avoid bumping into walls. To make these types of games, you'll learn to test for collisions.

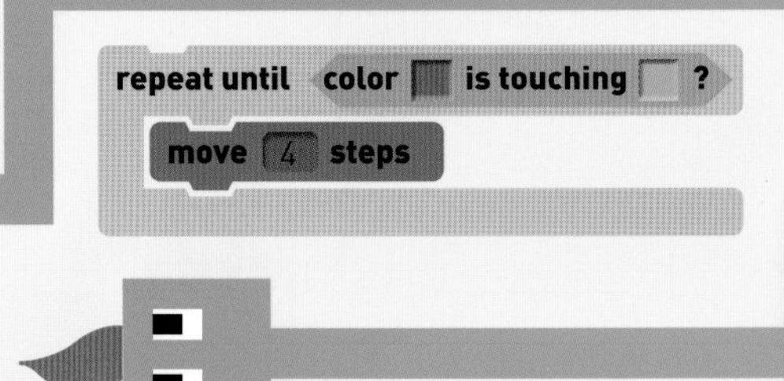

repeat until color is touching ?
move 4 steps

The Level 5 games will teach you how to code complex movements, using functions to make balls bounce and penguins jump.

A SCORE?

Score 12

That pizza is moving fast!

When you're playing a game, it's fun to see your score go higher and higher! In Level 2, you'll learn how to keep score using variables. You can use variables to store the number of lives left or the speed of a falling pizza . . .

COOL SPRITES?

The characters or objects that move around the screen, obeying your commands, are called sprites. Your sprite might be a hungry dog or a zappy spaceship. In the best games, sprites look exciting, scary, or funny.

In this book, you'll learn to draw your own sprites. In Level 3, you'll also learn to create animations, make the propeller on a plane go around, or make a cat look like it's walking.

```
repeat 3
    create clone of myself
```

Hello!

Hello!

Hello!

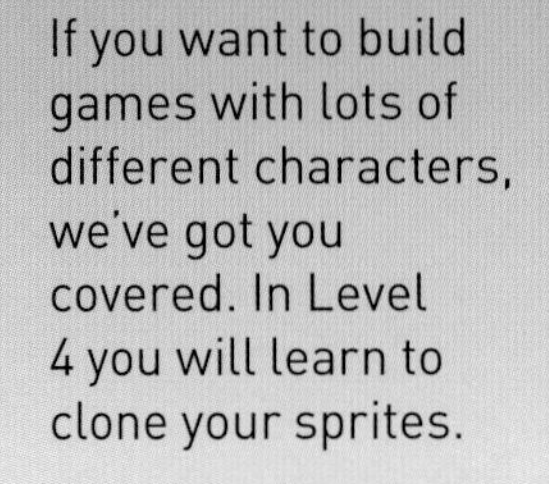

If you want to build games with lots of different characters, we've got you covered. In Level 4 you will learn to clone your sprites.

SOUND EFFECTS?

The best games not only look great but sound great as well. Using music and sound effects—like drum rolls and meowing cats—you'll give your games those essential finishing touches.

```
set instrument to 16
repeat 3
    play note 60 for 0.25 beats
    play note 64 for 0.1 beats
```

LEVEL BY LEVEL

The games in this book are divided into 5 levels. Like in a multi-level game, each level is a little harder than the last and builds on skills already learned. If you've never done any coding before, start at Level 1. By the time you make it to Level 5, you'll be an expert!

USING SCRATCH

There are many different computer languages and programs you can use to code games. In this book, we are using a simple yet powerful language called Scratch. It's free to use and easy to learn.

FINDING SCRATCH

To start using Scratch, open up a web browser and click in the address bar. Type in **scratch.mit.edu** then press **Return**, or **Enter**. Click **Try it out**.

STARTING SCRATCH

To code a computer game, you need to tell your computer exactly what to do by giving it commands. A command is an instruction to do a particular task. A program is a group of commands. In Scratch, commands are shown in the form of "code blocks." You build a game by choosing code blocks and then joining them together to create a program.

Your Scratch screen should look like this:

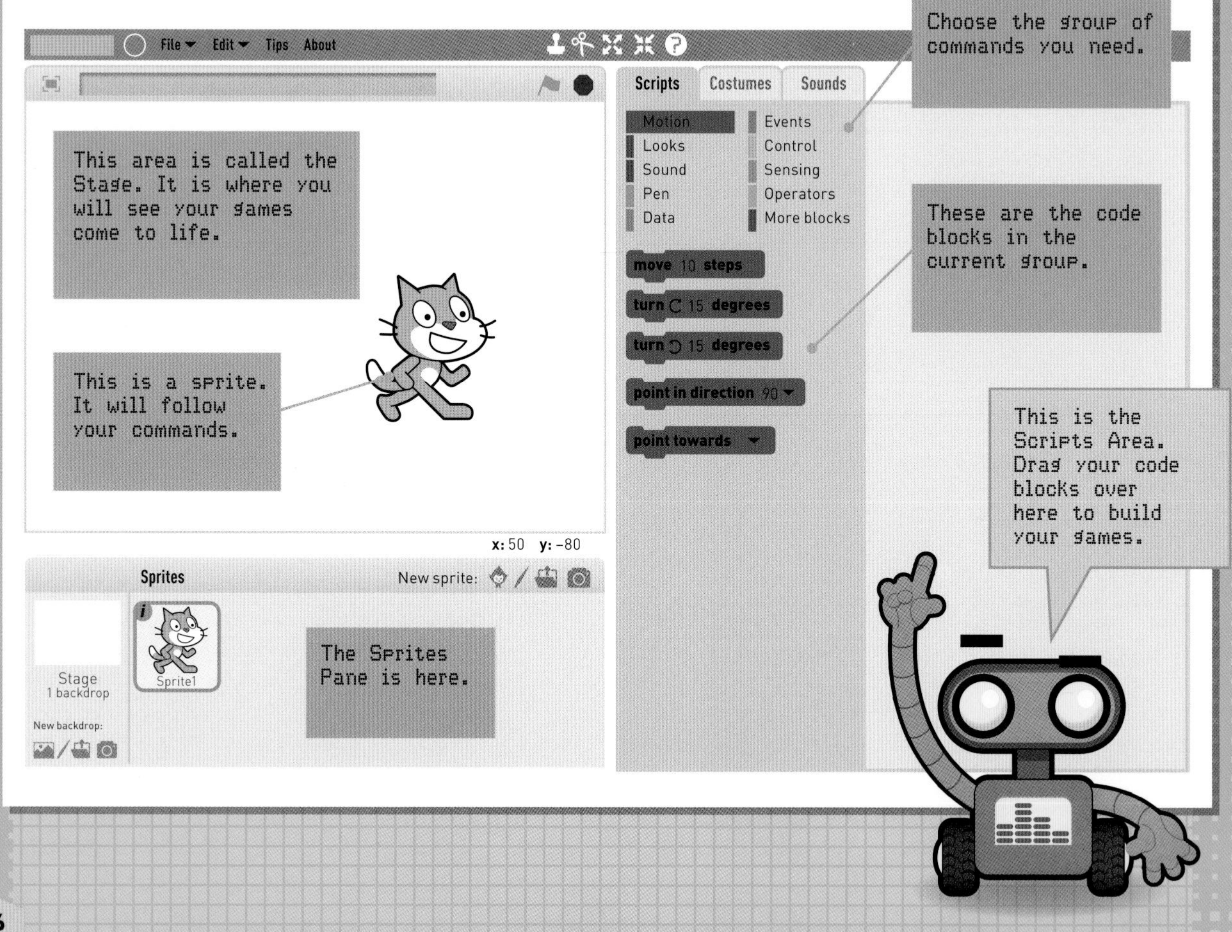

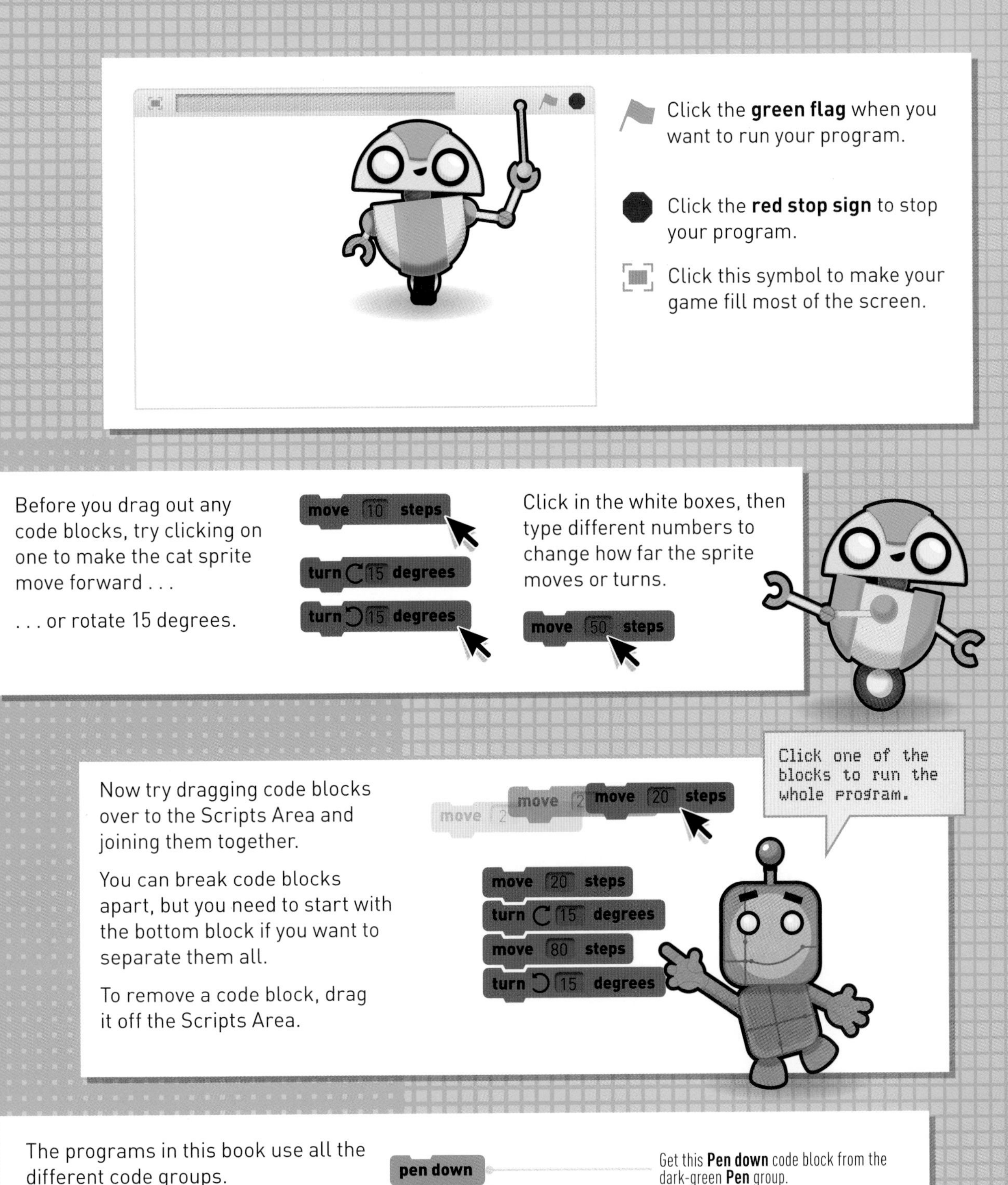
move 10 steps
turn 15 degrees
turn 15 degrees
move 50 steps
Click one of the blocks to run the whole program.
move 20 steps
move 20 steps
turn 15 degrees
move 80 steps
turn 15 degrees

Click the **green flag** when you want to run your program.

Click the **red stop sign** to stop your program.

Click this symbol to make your game fill most of the screen.

Before you drag out any code blocks, try clicking on one to make the cat sprite move forward . . .

. . . or rotate 15 degrees.

Click in the white boxes, then type different numbers to change how far the sprite moves or turns.

Now try dragging code blocks over to the Scripts Area and joining them together.

You can break code blocks apart, but you need to start with the bottom block if you want to separate them all.

To remove a code block, drag it off the Scripts Area.

The programs in this book use all the different code groups.

Use the color of the code blocks to figure out which group you will find the block in. It will also give you a clue about what the code block will do.

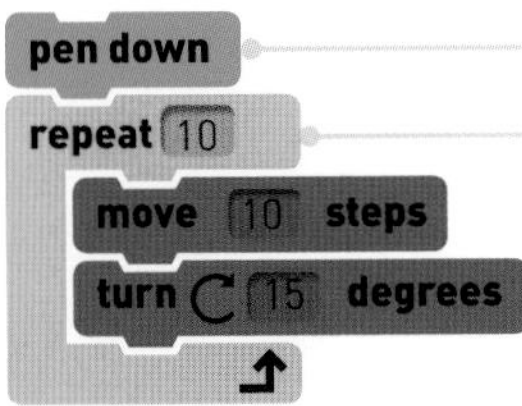
pen down
repeat 10
move 10 steps
turn 15 degrees

Get this **Pen down** code block from the dark-green **Pen** group.

The **Repeat** code block is a mustard color, so it will be in the **Control** group.

The dark-blue code blocks are all in the **Motion** group.

THE SPRITES PANE

The Sprites Pane shows which sprites are being used in a project. You can also use it to add a new sprite or to select the Stage.

The Stage is where you can draw or load backgrounds for your games. The Stage can't move around, but you can add code to it for things like sound effects.

Click this button to add a new sprite from the Library. The Library has ready-made sprites.

Click this button to design your own sprite.

Always make sure you add your code to the correct sprite or to the Stage!

USING THE DRAWING AREA

Lots of the games in this book give you the chance to make your own sprites and graphics. Don't be afraid to experiment and try out your own ideas, too. Here are some useful tips for using the Drawing Area.

To draw a new sprite, click on the **Paint new sprite** button located in the top bar of the Sprites Pane.

To draw a backdrop for the Stage, click on the **Stage** button located in the Sprites Pane, then click on **Paint new backdrop** underneath it.

The drawing area will appear on the right of your Scratch screen.

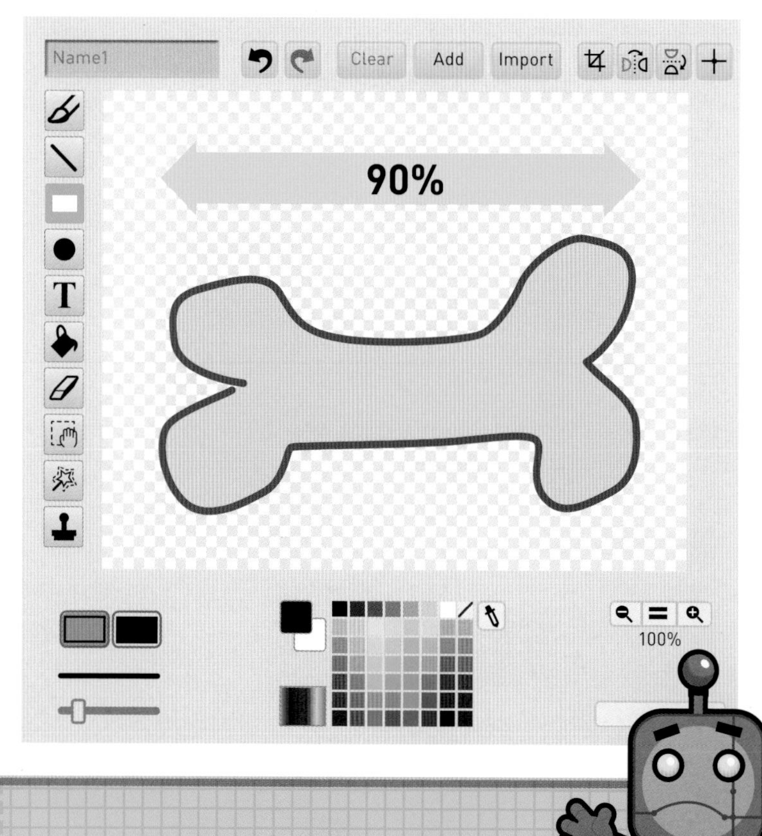

Sprite size

Usually, game designers draw large versions of their sprites so they can add detail, then shrink them by using a **Set size** code block from the **Looks** group. That is what we will do with our games.

To make the games work properly, you need to draw your sprites in the center of the drawing area. Your drawings should be as big as what is shown in this book. Watch out for the yellow arrows. If the yellow arrow says 90%, the picture should almost fill the drawing area.

If you notice the size of your sprite is wrong after you've coded a game, unfortunately the best option will be to redraw your sprite!

KEY DRAWING TOOLS

Brush
Use this for drawing.

Straight line
Tip: Hold down the Shift key to keep the line horizontal or vertical.

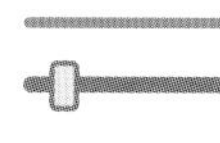

Options: Change the line thickness with the slider in the panel at the bottom.

Rectangle
Tip: Hold down the Shift key to make a square.

Ellipse (Oval)
Tip: Hold down the Shift key to make a circle.

Options: Choose to draw an outline or a solid shape.

Text
Use this for writing.

Font:
Arial ▾

Options: Choose your font style.

Flood fill
Fill the selected area.

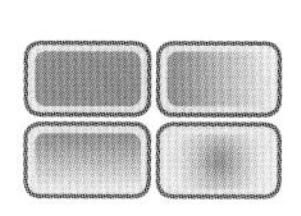

Options: Choose solid or gradient fill.

Undo and redo
When you make a mistake, don't reach for the eraser—click on "Undo" and try again!

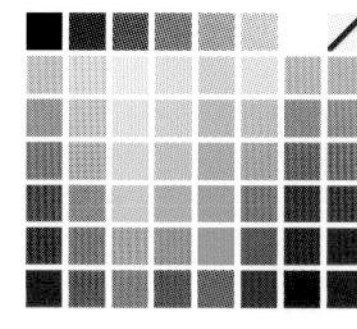

Colors
Pick colors to paint with.

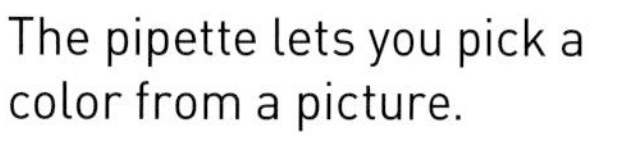

The pipette lets you pick a color from a picture.

Use this to adjust colors in detail.

Zoom in (+) and zoom out (–)
Zoom in to add detail or make sure things are lined up carefully. Zoom out to get an overview of how your sprite is developing. Remember, zooming doesn't make the actual sprite bigger or smaller—it just makes it look bigger or smaller (like a magnifying glass).

Select, move, and resize
If you draw something in the wrong place, the Select tool can fix it! Draw a blue box around part of a sprite. Put your mouse in the middle of the dotted box and drag to move that part of the sprite. Use the handles at the edge of the Select box to resize that part of your image.

STORING YOUR WORK

Click the **File** menu at the top of the screen on the left. Then click:
New to start some new work.
Download to your computer to save a file onto your computer.
Upload from your computer to open a file you have saved earlier.

new
download to your computer
upload from your computer

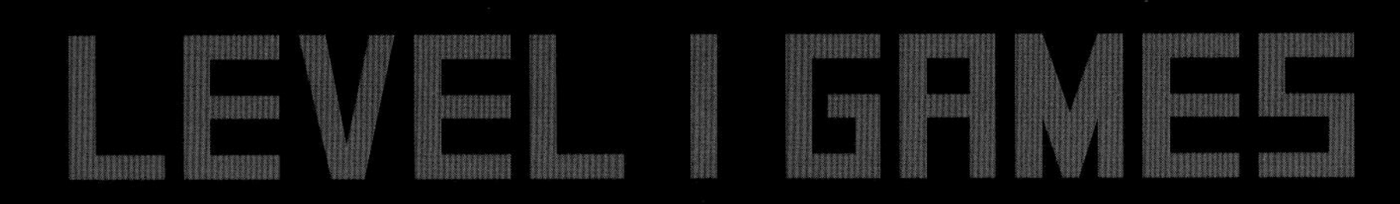

If you're a beginner at Scratch, these Level 1 games are a great starting point. They're simple to code but lots of fun to play. First of all, here are some explanations of key ideas you will come across in the Level 1 programs. Read through these pages before you start coding—or, if you can't wait, dive right in and check back here if you get stuck!

INPUTS AND MOVEMENT

There are two different ways to control sprites in the Level 1 games: using the mouse or using the keyboard.

In *Hungry Cat* (page 12) and *Treasure Island* (page 14), the player guides the cat sprite around the screen by pointing with the mouse.

The cat points in the right direction because we use the **Point towards** block.

MOUSE

point towards mouse-pointer

move 4 steps

The games *Amazing Maze* (page 16), *Tunnel of Gold* (page 22), and *Cross the Road* (page 24) work with keyboard inputs. An input is an action that tells a computer to do something. When different keys are pressed, different pieces of code run that move the sprite in a particular direction.

Drive Me Crazy (page 18) also uses **Turn** code blocks. These rotate the car when a key is pressed.

KEYBOARD

when right arrow key pressed
point in direction 90
move 5 steps

turn C 10 degrees

LOOPS AND REPETITION

To make sure code keeps running during a game, we usually put it inside a **Forever** block—that way the game will never stop. This is called a loop. Adding a loop makes a set of commands repeat over and over.

Some games use a **Repeat until** loop. These loops keep repeating until something happens. In *Cross the Road* (page 24), we use a **Repeat until** loop to keep the cars racing down the road—until they hit our cat sprite!

If you want a command to keep on repeating, put that code block inside the "C" shape of the "Forever" block.

IF, COLLISION, AND TOUCHING COLORS

When something happens in a game, such as one sprite catching another, we need to run a different piece of code. For example, in *Hungry Cat* (page 12), if the cat touches an apple, we want that apple to disappear, as if it's been eaten.

We do this using an **If** code block. This code runs inside each apple. If the cat touches the apple, then the code block inside the **If** loop runs . . . and the apple disappears.

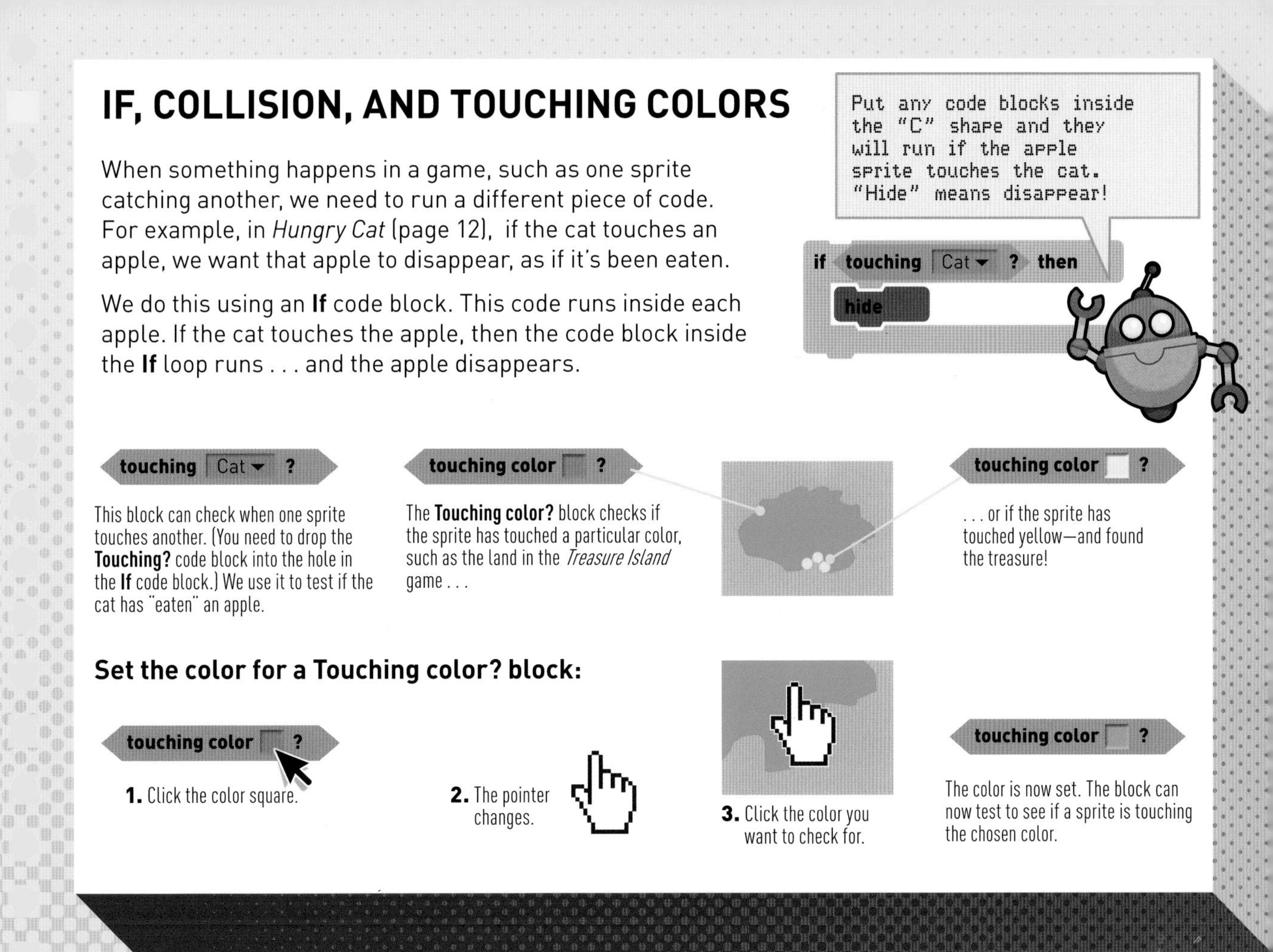

Put any code blocks inside the "C" shape and they will run if the apple sprite touches the cat. "Hide" means disappear!
if touching Cat ? then
hide
touching Cat ?
touching color ?
touching color ?
touching color ?
touching color ?

This block can check when one sprite touches another. (You need to drop the **Touching?** code block into the hole in the **If** code block.) We use it to test if the cat has "eaten" an apple.

The **Touching color?** block checks if the sprite has touched a particular color, such as the land in the *Treasure Island* game . . .

. . . or if the sprite has touched yellow—and found the treasure!

Set the color for a Touching color? block:

1. Click the color square.

2. The pointer changes.

3. Click the color you want to check for.

The color is now set. The block can now test to see if a sprite is touching the chosen color.

COORDINATES: SETTING X AND Y

Sometimes we need to move sprites to particular places on the screen at the start of a game. In *Cross the Road* (page 24) and *Tunnel of Gold* (page 22), we do this by setting the coordinates of the cat sprite.

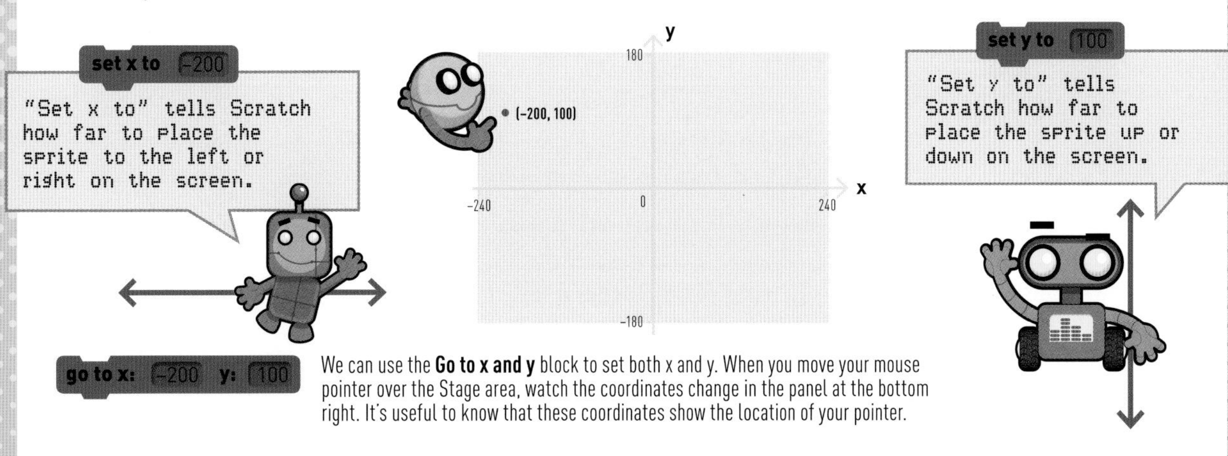

set x to -200
"Set x to" tells Scratch how far to place the sprite to the left or right on the screen.

set y to 100
"Set y to" tells Scratch how far to place the sprite up or down on the screen.
go to x: -200 y: 100

We can use the **Go to x and y** block to set both x and y. When you move your mouse pointer over the Stage area, watch the coordinates change in the panel at the bottom right. It's useful to know that these coordinates show the location of your pointer.

HUNGRY CAT

For our first game, a cat sprite will move around the screen gobbling up apples. The player controls the cat by pointing to a place on the screen using the mouse. The cat then moves toward it. If the cat touches one of the apples, the apple disappears—as if it's been eaten up!

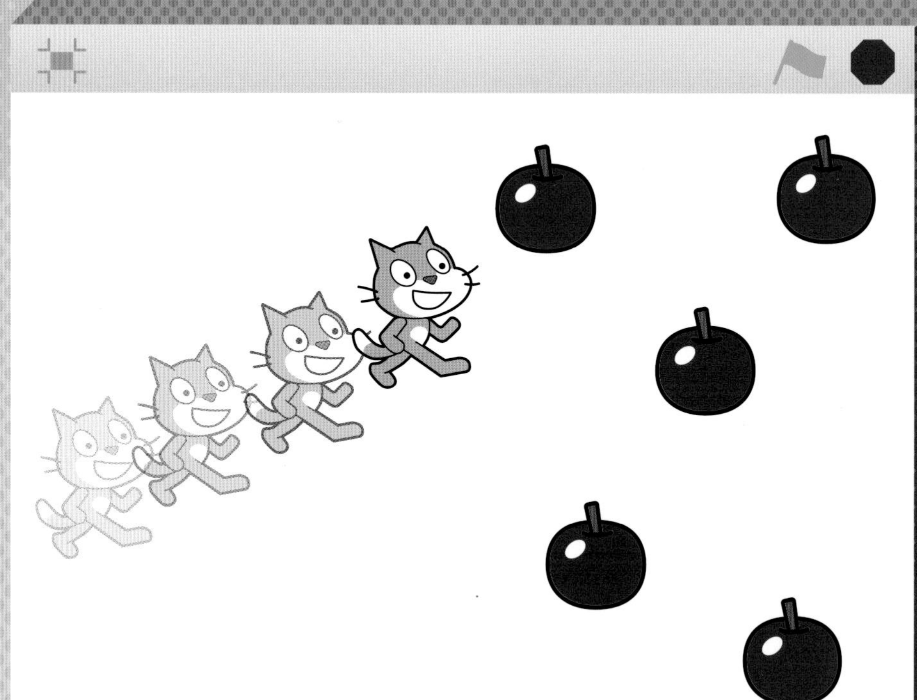

1

Start a new Scratch file, then drag these code blocks to the Scripts Area. The **When green flag clicked** block is in the **Events** group, the **Forever** block is in the **Control** group, and you'll find the other blocks in the **Motion** group.

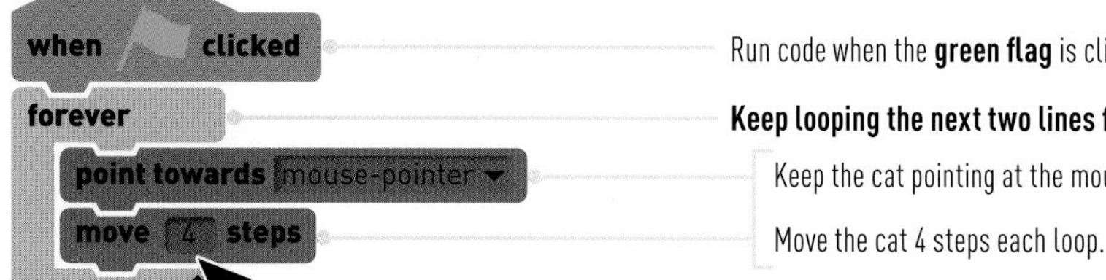

Run code when the **green flag** is clicked.

Keep looping the next two lines forever:

Keep the cat pointing at the mouse.

Move the cat 4 steps each loop.

Change the **Point towards** drop-down menu to say **Mouse-pointer**. Change the number of steps to move to **4**.

2

Click the **green flag** at the top right of the Stage to test your code so far. Move the mouse around and watch the cat move toward it. If it doesn't work, check your code to make sure it matches the blocks above.

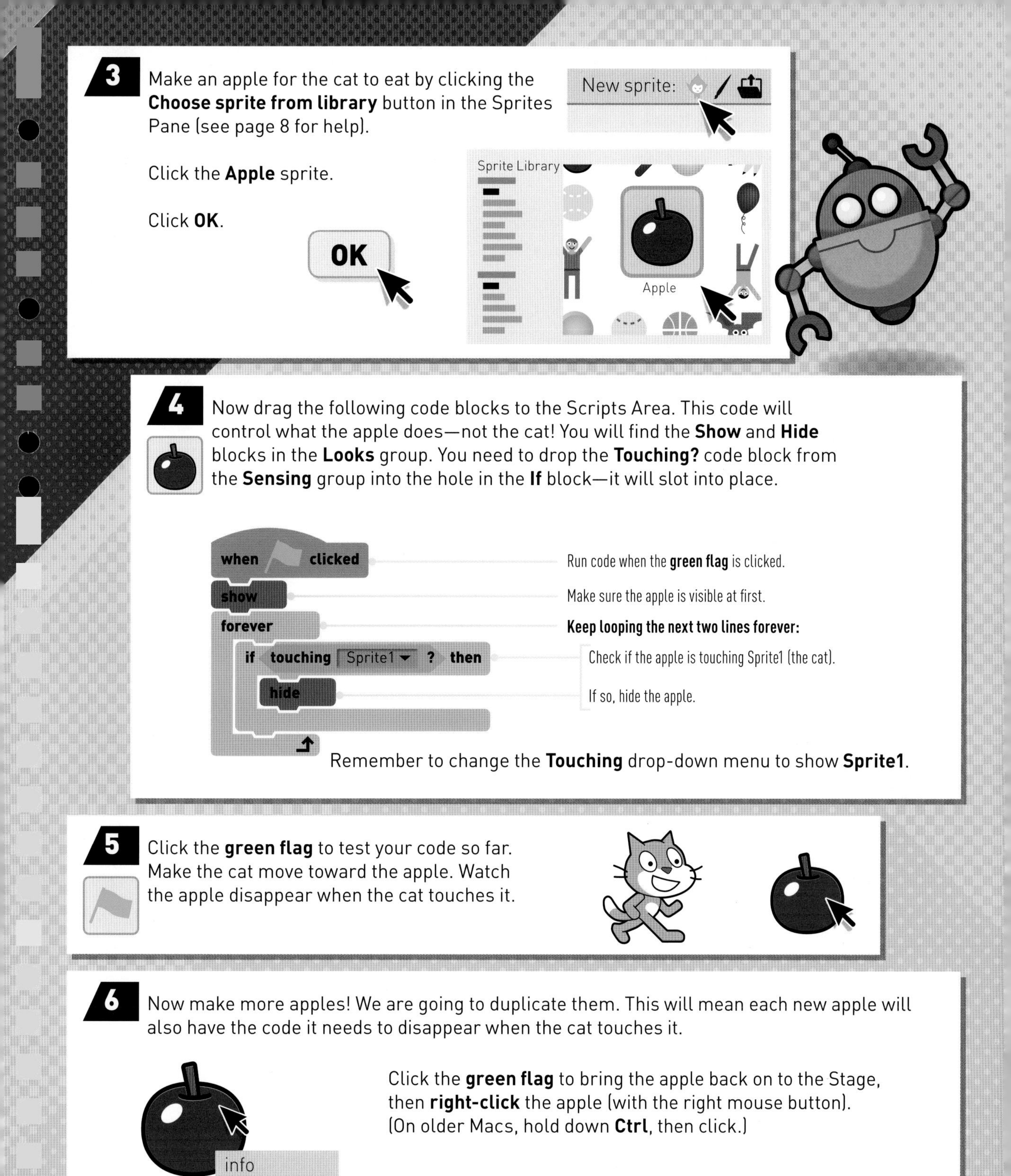

3 Make an apple for the cat to eat by clicking the **Choose sprite from library** button in the Sprites Pane (see page 8 for help).

Click the **Apple** sprite.

Click **OK**.

4 Now drag the following code blocks to the Scripts Area. This code will control what the apple does—not the cat! You will find the **Show** and **Hide** blocks in the **Looks** group. You need to drop the **Touching?** code block from the **Sensing** group into the hole in the **If** block—it will slot into place.

```
when [flag] clicked
show
forever
    if touching Sprite1 ? then
        hide
```

- when clicked: Run code when the **green flag** is clicked.
- show: Make sure the apple is visible at first.
- forever: **Keep looping the next two lines forever:**
  - if touching Sprite1 ? then: Check if the apple is touching Sprite1 (the cat).
  - hide: If so, hide the apple.

Remember to change the **Touching** drop-down menu to show **Sprite1**.

5 Click the **green flag** to test your code so far. Make the cat move toward the apple. Watch the apple disappear when the cat touches it.

6 Now make more apples! We are going to duplicate them. This will mean each new apple will also have the code it needs to disappear when the cat touches it.

Click the **green flag** to bring the apple back on to the Stage, then **right-click** the apple (with the right mouse button). (On older Macs, hold down **Ctrl**, then click.)

Then click **Duplicate**. Drag your new apple into a space on the Stage. Test your code, then add another apple or two. Have fun playing your first game!

TREASURE ISLAND

In this game, the player has to sail their pirate ship around an island to reach the treasure. The game ends if the boat hits the island or finds the treasure. We will program this by looking for the colors the boat touches—green or yellow. We will also learn how to draw a background.

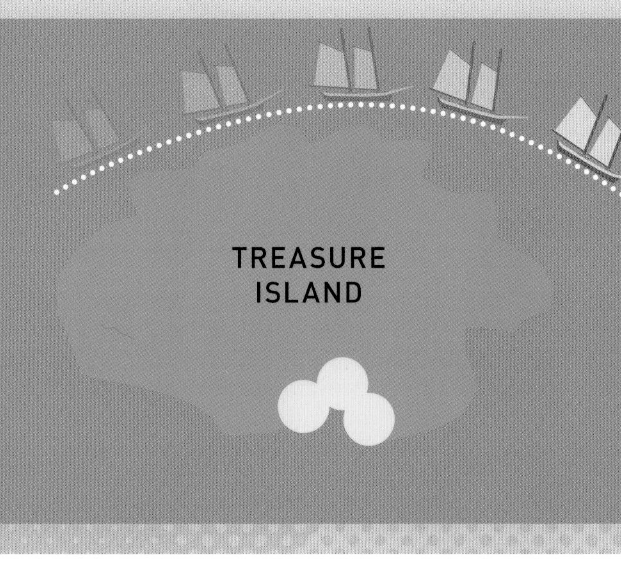

1 Start a new Scratch file. Delete the cat sprite first:

Find the Sprites Pane at the bottom left of the screen. See page 8 for help.

Right-click the cat sprite with the right mouse button. (On older Macs, hold down the **Ctrl** key, then click.)

Click **Delete**.

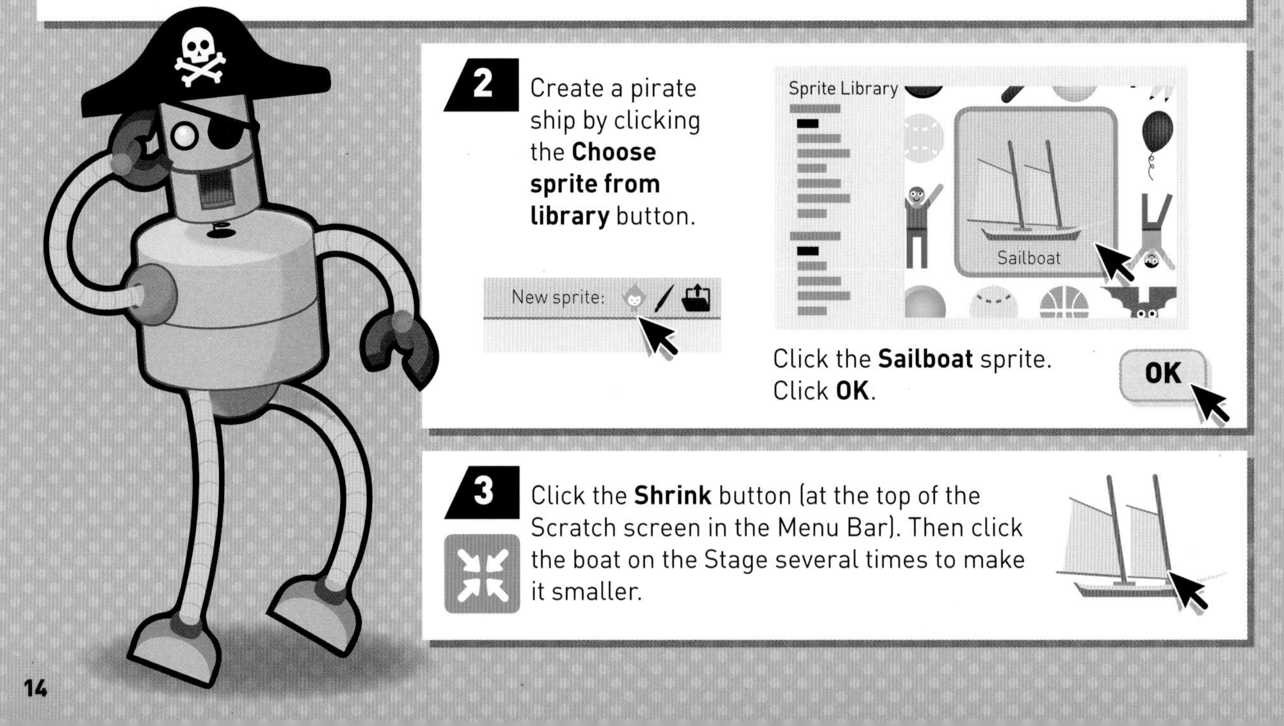

2 Create a pirate ship by clicking the **Choose sprite from library** button.

Click the **Sailboat** sprite. Click **OK**.

3 Click the **Shrink** button (at the top of the Scratch screen in the Menu Bar). Then click the boat on the Stage several times to make it smaller.

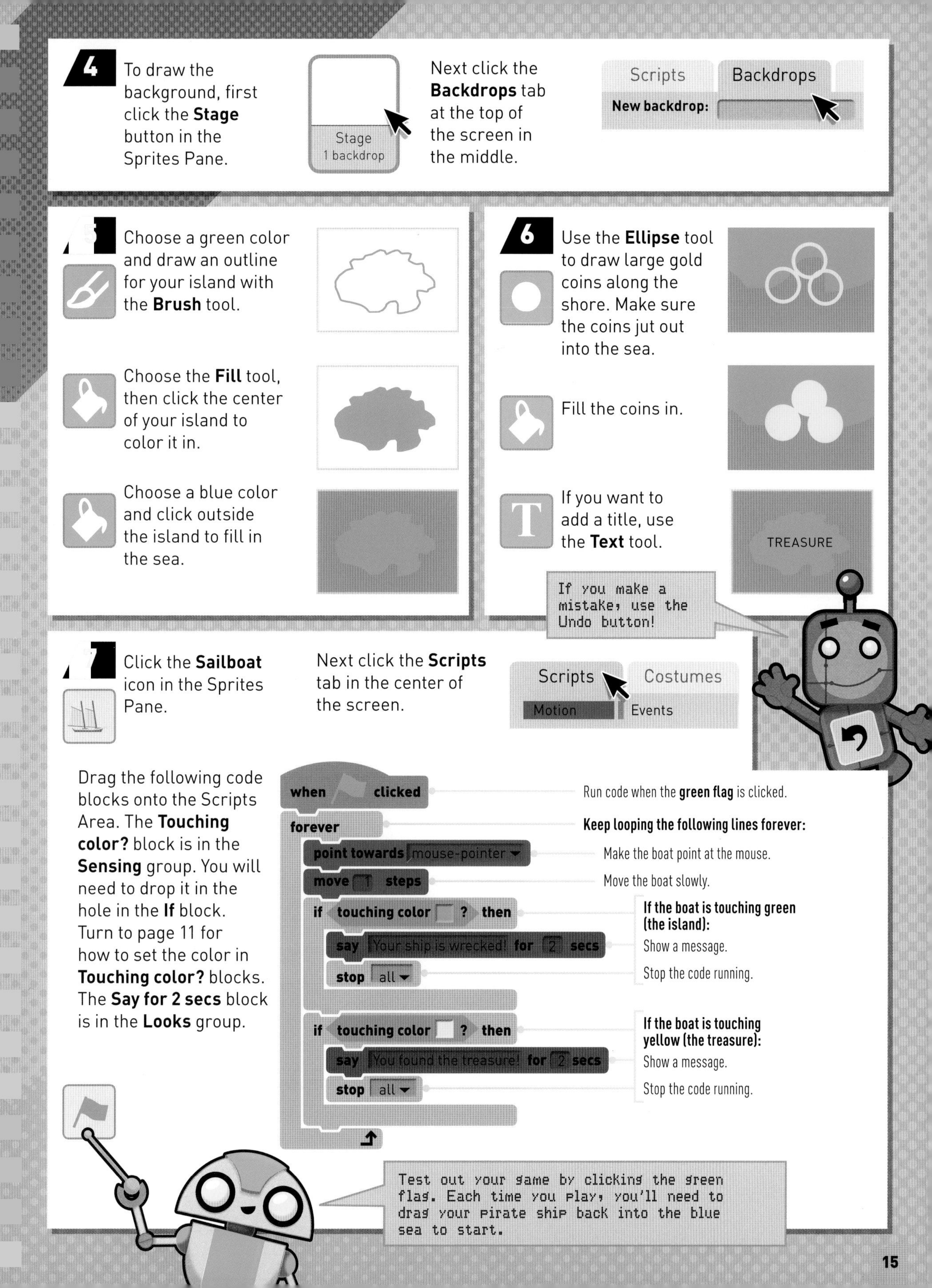

4 To draw the background, first click the **Stage** button in the Sprites Pane.

Next click the **Backdrops** tab at the top of the screen in the middle.

5 Choose a green color and draw an outline for your island with the **Brush** tool.

Choose the **Fill** tool, then click the center of your island to color it in.

Choose a blue color and click outside the island to fill in the sea.

6 Use the **Ellipse** tool to draw large gold coins along the shore. Make sure the coins jut out into the sea.

Fill the coins in.

If you want to add a title, use the **Text** tool.

TREASURE

If you make a mistake, use the Undo button!

7 Click the **Sailboat** icon in the Sprites Pane.

Next click the **Scripts** tab in the center of the screen.

Drag the following code blocks onto the Scripts Area. The **Touching color?** block is in the **Sensing** group. You will need to drop it in the hole in the **If** block. Turn to page 11 for how to set the color in **Touching color?** blocks. The **Say for 2 secs** block is in the **Looks** group.

```
when [flag] clicked                          Run code when the green flag is clicked.
forever                                      Keep looping the following lines forever:
    point towards [mouse-pointer]            Make the boat point at the mouse.
    move (1) steps                           Move the boat slowly.
    if <touching color [ ] ?> then           If the boat is touching green (the island):
        say [Your ship is wrecked!] for (2) secs    Show a message.
        stop [all]                           Stop the code running.
    if <touching color [ ] ?> then           If the boat is touching yellow (the treasure):
        say [You found the treasure!] for (2) secs  Show a message.
        stop [all]                           Stop the code running.
```

Test out your game by clicking the green flag. Each time you play, you'll need to drag your pirate ship back into the blue sea to start.

AMAZING MAZE

In this fun maze game, we are going to move the sprite around by using "key press events." When the Up arrow key is pressed, the sprite will move up. To stop the sprite when it hits a wall, we will test for the color it is touching.

1 Start a new Scratch file. Click the **Shrink** button at the top of the screen, then click the cat on the Stage several times to make it smaller.

2 To draw the background, first click the **Stage** button in the Sprites Pane.

Next click the **Backdrops** tab at the top of the screen in the middle.

3 Choose the **Rectangle** tool.

At the bottom of the screen, click the shaded rectangle so your rectangles will be colored in.

4 Start making your maze by dragging out rectangles.

If you make a mistake, use the **Eraser** or click **Undo**.

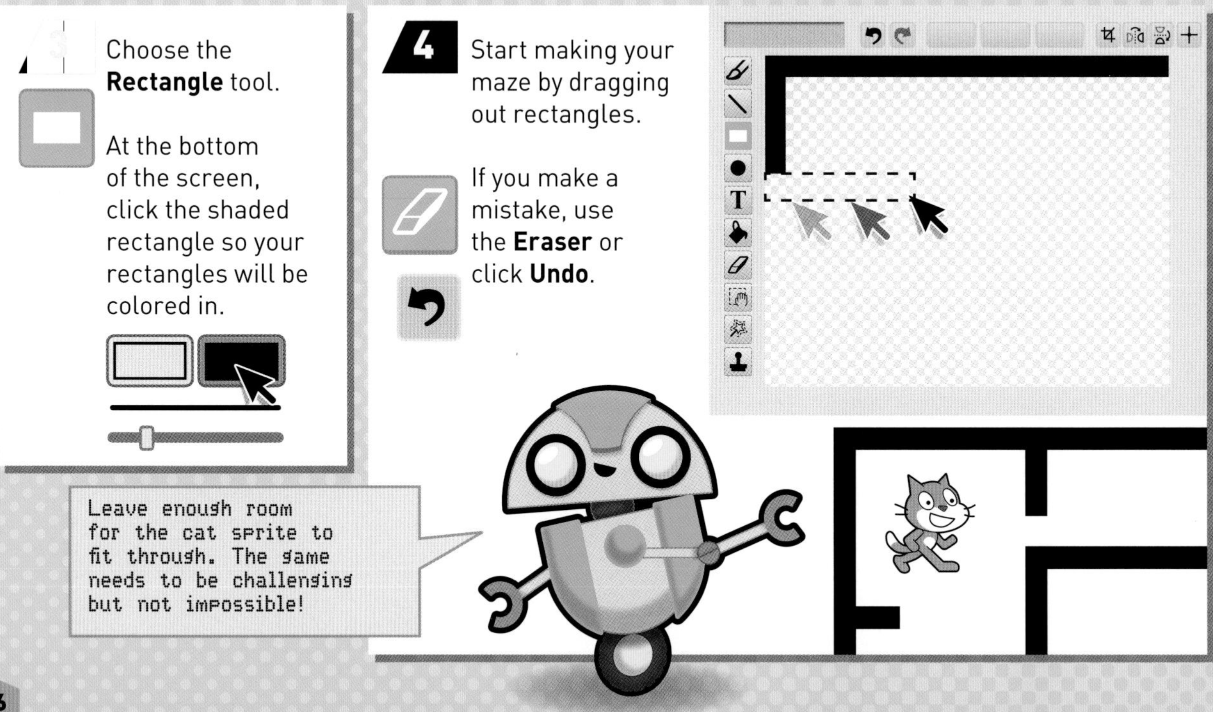

Leave enough room for the cat sprite to fit through. The game needs to be challenging but not impossible!

5

To add code to the cat sprite, click on **Sprite1** in the Sprites Pane.

Next click the **Scripts** tab.

Now drag in the following code. The **When key pressed** blocks are in the **Events** group.

```
when up arrow key pressed
point in direction 0
move 10 steps
```

Run this code while the Up arrow is pressed:
- Point upward (0 degrees). You need to click the drop-down menu to set this.
- Move the cat sprite 10 steps.

```
when down arrow key pressed
point in direction 180
move 10 steps
```

Run this code while the Down arrow is pressed:
- Point down (180 degrees).
- Move the cat sprite 10 steps.

```
when left arrow key pressed
point in direction -90
move 10 steps
```

Run this code while the Left arrow is pressed:
- Point left (–90 degrees).
- Move the cat sprite 10 steps.

```
when right arrow key pressed
point in direction 90
move 10 steps
```

Run this code while the Right arrow is pressed:
- Point right (90 degrees).
- Move the cat sprite 10 steps.

6

Click the **green flag** to test your code so far. The cat should move around when you press the arrow keys—but at this stage it can walk through walls!

7

To stop the cat when it hits a wall, drag in the following code. For help setting the **Touching color?** block, turn to page 11.

```
when green flag clicked
forever
  if touching color [black] ? then
    turn C 180 degrees
    move 10 steps
```

Run code when the **green flag** is pressed.

Keep running this code forever:

Check if the cat is touching black (the walls):
- If it is, then turn around.
- Move 10 steps (move back).

Click the green flag to test your game!

DRIVE ME CRAZY

This driving game is simple to code and lots of fun to play! Instead of using four keys to move in four different directions, the Left and Right arrow keys are used to rotate the car left or right. The space bar is used to move it forward in a loop. If the car sprite senses it is touching green, it stops.

1 Start a new Scratch file. Delete the cat sprite first:

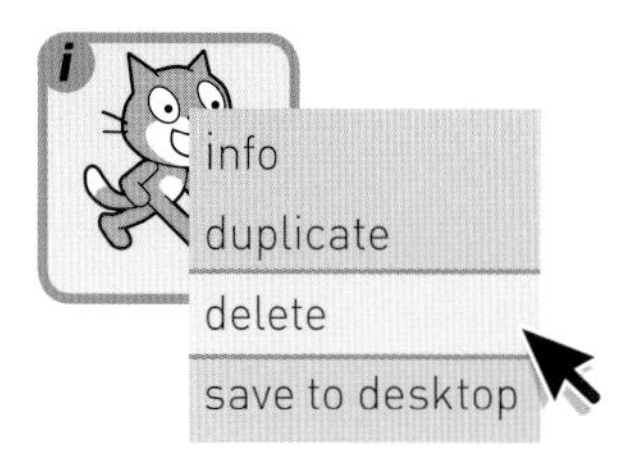

Right-click the **Sprite1** button with the right mouse button. (On older Macs, hold the **Ctrl** key, then click.) Click **Delete**.

2 Draw your car by clicking the **Paint new sprite** button. We will draw it as if it's viewed from above.

New sprite:

Choose the **Rectangle** tool.

At the bottom of the screen, click the shaded rectangle.

Choose red.

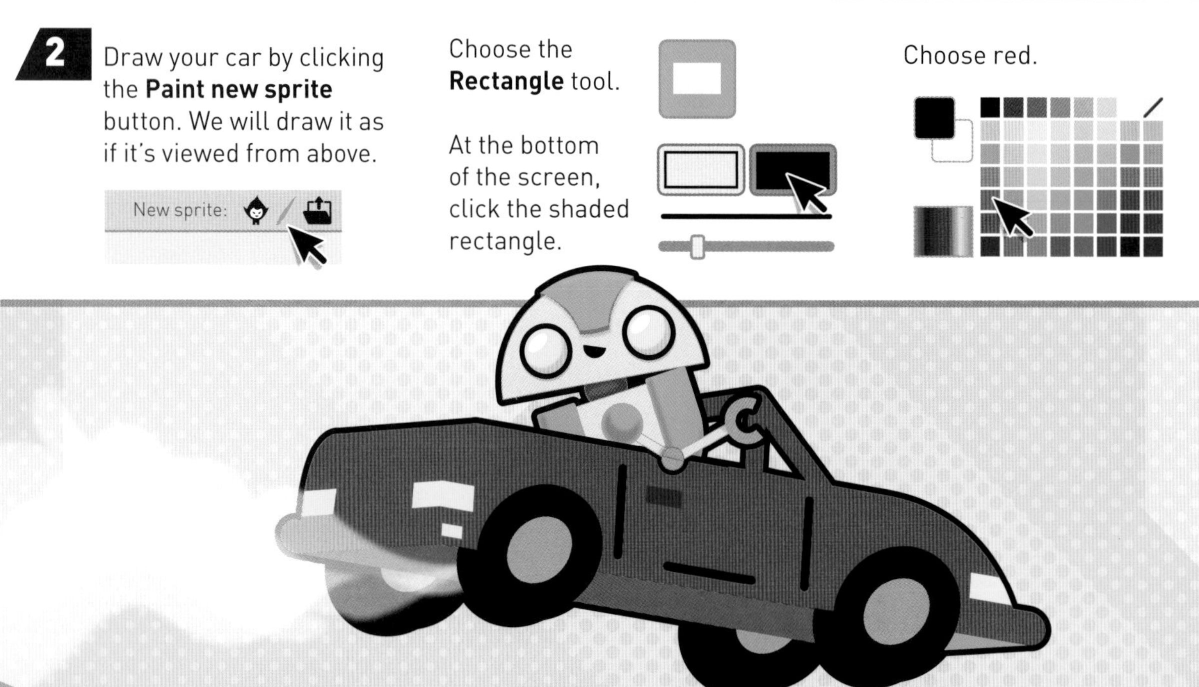

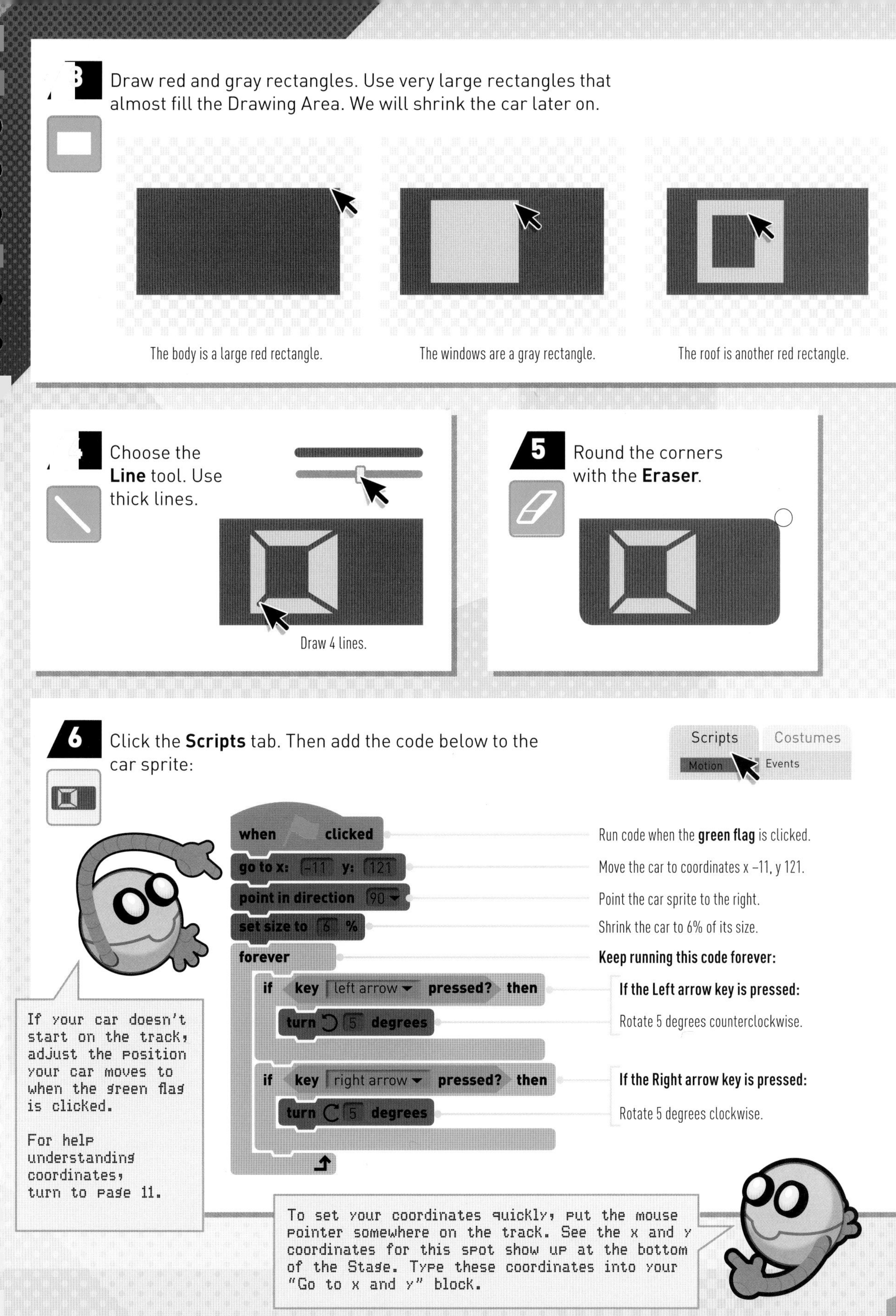

3

Draw red and gray rectangles. Use very large rectangles that almost fill the Drawing Area. We will shrink the car later on.

The body is a large red rectangle.

The windows are a gray rectangle.

The roof is another red rectangle.

4

Choose the **Line** tool. Use thick lines.

Draw 4 lines.

5

Round the corners with the **Eraser**.

6

Click the **Scripts** tab. Then add the code below to the car sprite:


```
when [green flag] clicked
go to x: -11 y: 121
point in direction 90
set size to 6 %
forever
    if key left arrow pressed? then
        turn ↺ 5 degrees
    if key right arrow pressed? then
        turn ↻ 5 degrees
```

Run code when the **green flag** is clicked.

Move the car to coordinates x –11, y 121.

Point the car sprite to the right.

Shrink the car to 6% of its size.

Keep running this code forever:

If the Left arrow key is pressed:

Rotate 5 degrees counterclockwise.

If the Right arrow key is pressed:

Rotate 5 degrees clockwise.

If your car doesn't start on the track, adjust the position your car moves to when the green flag is clicked.

For help understanding coordinates, turn to page 11.

To set your coordinates quickly, put the mouse pointer somewhere on the track. See the x and y coordinates for this spot show up at the bottom of the Stage. Type these coordinates into your "Go to x and y" block.

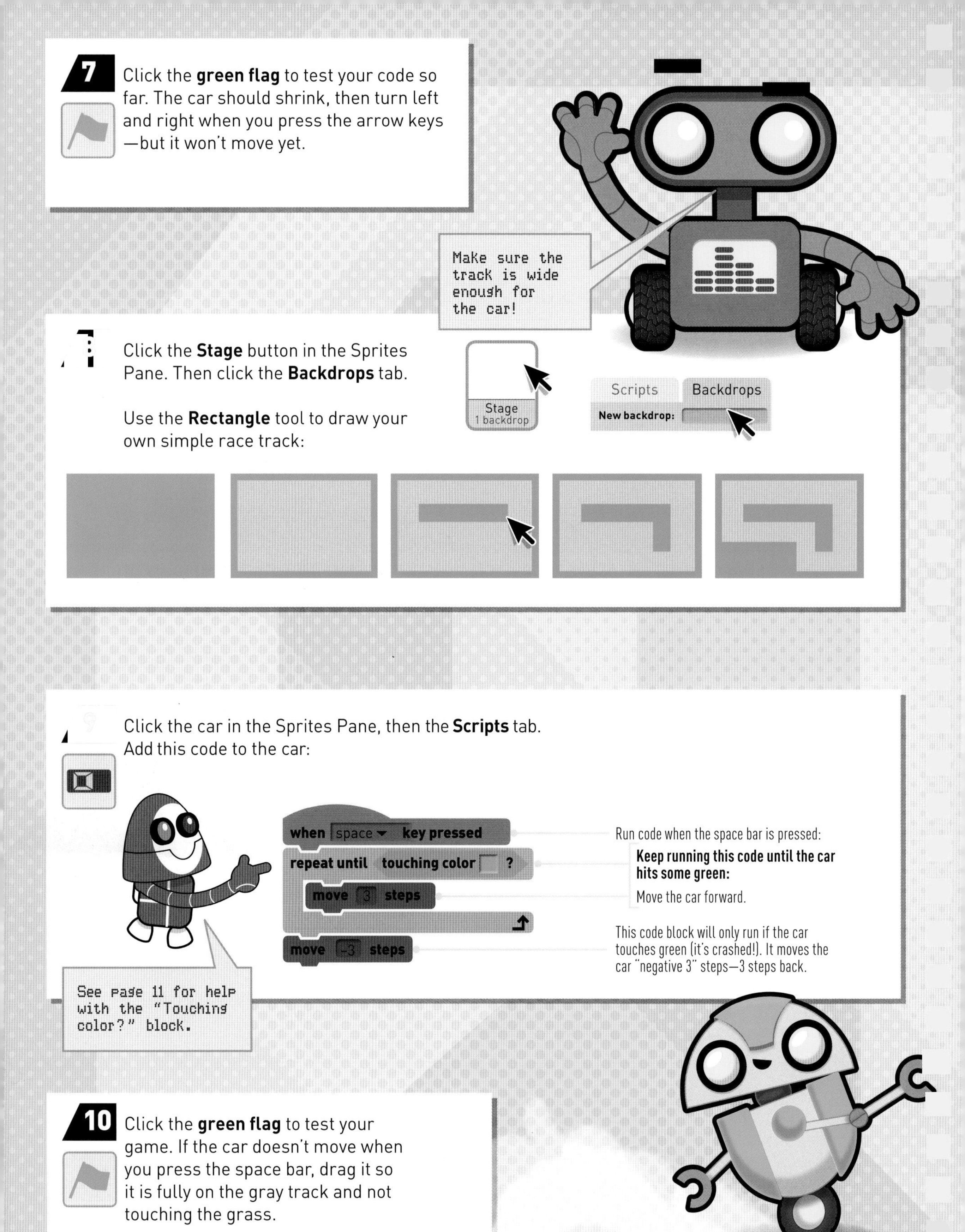

Make sure the track is wide enough for the car!
See page 11 for help with the "Touching color?" block.
Stage
1 backdrop
Scripts
Backdrops
New backdrop:

7 Click the **green flag** to test your code so far. The car should shrink, then turn left and right when you press the arrow keys—but it won't move yet.

8 Click the **Stage** button in the Sprites Pane. Then click the **Backdrops** tab.

Use the **Rectangle** tool to draw your own simple race track:

9 Click the car in the Sprites Pane, then the **Scripts** tab. Add this code to the car:

```
when [space ▾] key pressed
repeat until <touching color [ ] ?>
    move (3) steps
end
move (-3) steps
```

Run code when the space bar is pressed:

Keep running this code until the car hits some green:

Move the car forward.

This code block will only run if the car touches green (it's crashed!). It moves the car "negative 3" steps—3 steps back.

10 Click the **green flag** to test your game. If the car doesn't move when you press the space bar, drag it so it is fully on the gray track and not touching the grass.

CHALLENGES

- Draw some spectators, trees, or patterns in the background. Don't let them interfere with how your game works, though!
- Add a sound effect from the **Sounds** group if your car leaves the track. Hint: You'll need to add a code block below the **Move -3 steps** block in step 9.
- Add a button that acts as a brake to stop the car when you press it.
- Add a small patch of oil to the track. Add a loop that runs forever and checks to see if the car has touched the color of the oil. How can you make the car skid when it hits this color?
- Duplicate the **When space key pressed** code (in step 9) so you have a "go faster" button. Change the code so it runs when you press a different key.
- Add a second car to make it a two-player game. Choose different keys to control the second car.

EXPERIMENT

- Try changing the angle the car turns when you press the **Left** and **Right** arrow keys (it is currently set to turn 5 degrees—see step 6). See what happens if you put in 1 degree or 15 degrees.

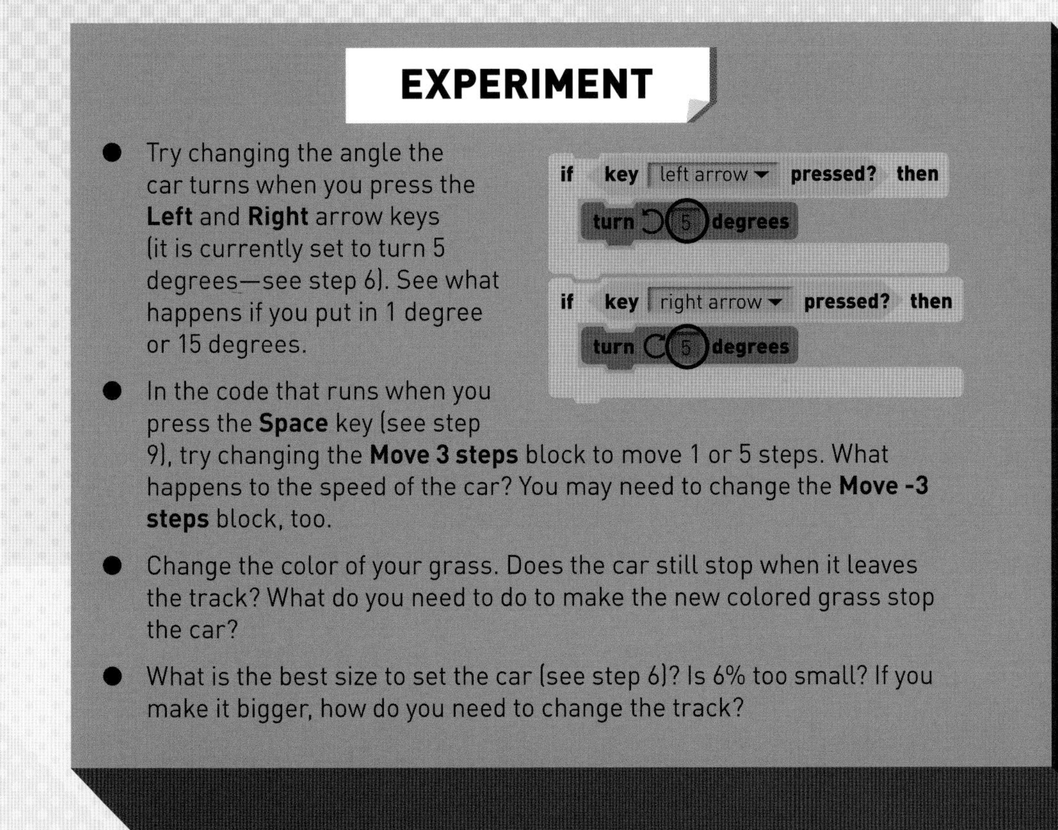

if key left arrow pressed? then
turn 5 degrees
if key right arrow pressed? then
turn 5 degrees

- In the code that runs when you press the **Space** key (see step 9), try changing the **Move 3 steps** block to move 1 or 5 steps. What happens to the speed of the car? You may need to change the **Move -3 steps** block, too.
- Change the color of your grass. Does the car still stop when it leaves the track? What do you need to do to make the new colored grass stop the car?
- What is the best size to set the car (see step 6)? Is 6% too small? If you make it bigger, how do you need to change the track?

TUNNEL OF GOLD

This game works the same way as *Amazing Maze* (page 16) but includes some exciting extra features, such as sound effects. The cat sprite moves to the starting coordinates automatically and will know it's reached the gold by checking for the color yellow.

A timer checks how long it takes the player to reach the gold.

1 Click the **Shrink** button at the top of the screen, then click the cat sprite several times to make it much smaller.

2 To draw the background, click the **Stage** button in the Sprites Pane. Click the **Backdrops** tab at the top of the screen in the middle.

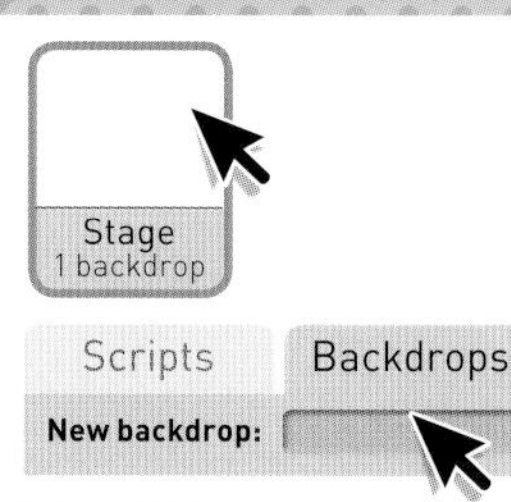
Stage
1 backdrop
Scripts
Backdrops
New backdrop:

3 Draw an underground maze like the one above, using the techniques shown on page 16, steps 3 and 4. Use dark brown for the walls. Use yellow to draw the gold, using the **Ellipse** tool and the techniques shown on page 15, step 6. Make sure the cat sprite fits through all the gaps.

4 To add code to the cat sprite, click on it in the Sprites Pane. Next click the **Scripts** tab.

Add the following code to make the cat sprite move:

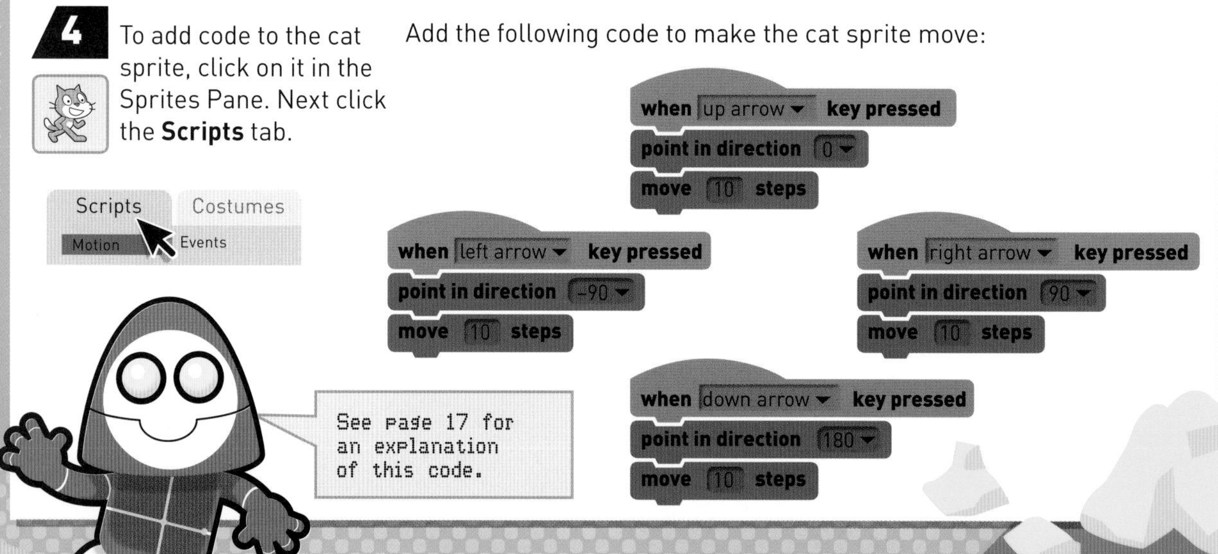
Scripts
Costumes
Motion
Events
when up arrow key pressed
point in direction 0
move 10 steps
when left arrow key pressed
point in direction -90
move 10 steps
when right arrow key pressed
point in direction 90
move 10 steps
when down arrow key pressed
point in direction 180
move 10 steps
See page 17 for an explanation of this code.

5

Add the following code to the cat sprite. The **Set instrument** and **Play note** blocks are in the **Sound** group. The **Timer** blocks are in the **Sensing** group. To make the program show the time taken, you will need to drop the little **Timer** block on top of the **Say hello** block from the **Looks** group.

For help with setting the colors for the "Touching color?" blocks, turn to page 11.

```
when [green flag] clicked                      Run code when the green flag is clicked.
reset timer                                    Reset the timer at the start of the game.
set instrument to (18)                         Select instrument 18, the steel drums.
play note (72) for (0.5) beats                 Play a C note for half a beat.
go to x: (-223) y: (-146)                      Move the cat to the start of the tunnel.
                                               Turn to page 11 for help with coordinates.
point in direction (90)                        Point to the right.
repeat until <touching color [yellow]?>        Run this code until the cat touches yellow (the gold):
  if <touching color [dark brown]?> then         If the cat is touching dark-brown earth (the walls):
    turn (180) degrees                             Turn 180 degrees (the opposite direction).
    move (10) steps                                Move 10 steps (move back).
    play drum (2) for (0.05) beats                 And make a bang (drum sound).
                                               This code runs when the player reaches the gold:
say (timer)                                    Show the timer—how long the player has taken.
play note (60) for (0.5) beats
play note (64) for (0.5) beats                 Play a short tune of four notes, C, E, G, C.
play note (67) for (0.5) beats
play note (72) for (0.5) beats
```

6

Test your game by clicking the **green flag**. You will need to adjust the position your cat sprite starts from by changing the x and y coordinates in the **Go to x and y** block. Turn to page 19 for help.

EXPERIMENT

Try changing the instrument number and see how it changes the tune.

Using the drop-down menus, see what happens if you change the note and beats.

play note 60 for 0.5 beats

Middle C (60)

CHALLENGES

The timer works with two lines of code:

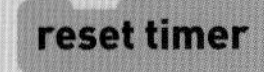

1. When the program starts, the timer is set to 0, just like a stopwatch.

say timer

2. This doesn't stop the timer, but shows how long it has been running, or the time taken so far in search of the gold.

Now turn to page 14 and remake *Treasure Island*. Add a timer that shows how long it takes the player to find the treasure.

CROSS THE ROAD

In this game, the cat sprite has to cross the road while avoiding the speeding cars. We are going to animate the cat as it walks to bring it to life. The cars move in a different way from sprites in previous games, bouncing off the edge of the Stage. We will use a special method called broadcasting to send a message from the car to the cat.

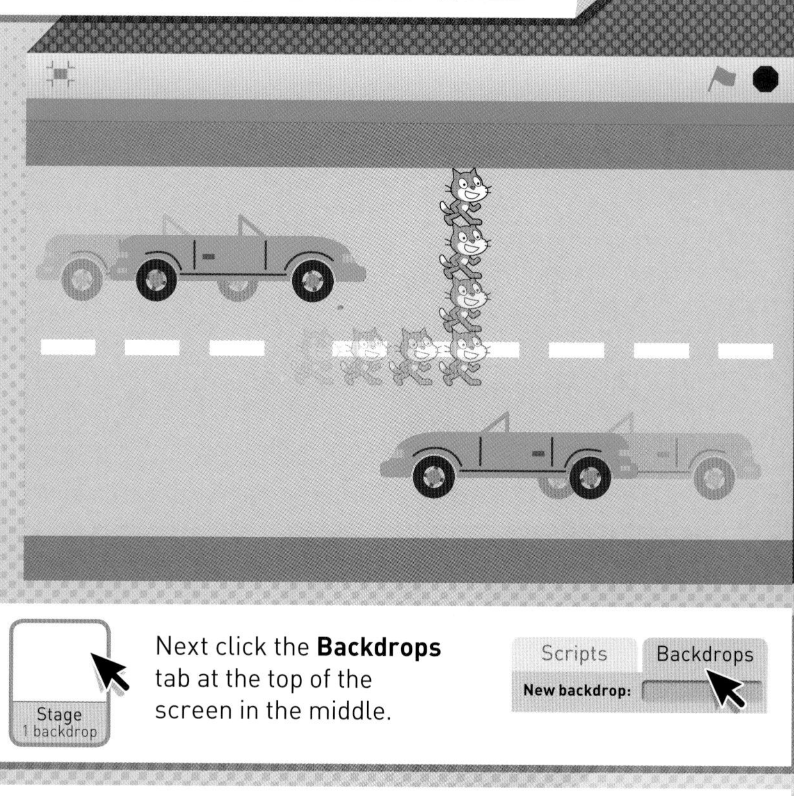

1 To draw the background, click the **Stage** button in the Sprites Pane.

Stage
1 backdrop

Next click the **Backdrops** tab at the top of the screen in the middle.

Scripts Backdrops
New backdrop:

2 Choose the **Rectangle** tool.

At the bottom of the screen, click the shaded rectangle so your rectangles are colored in.

Draw dark-gray, light-gray, green, and white rectangles:

Pavement | The road | Some grass | Road markings

3 Click the cat sprite in the Sprites Pane, then the **Scripts** tab. Add this code:

Make sure you add code for each of the four directions.

```
when [up arrow] key pressed
point in direction (0)
```

```
when [left arrow] key pressed
point in direction (-90)
```

```
when [right arrow] key pressed
point in direction (90)
```

```
when [down arrow] key pressed
point in direction (180)
```

Run this code while the Down arrow is pressed:

Point down (180 degrees).

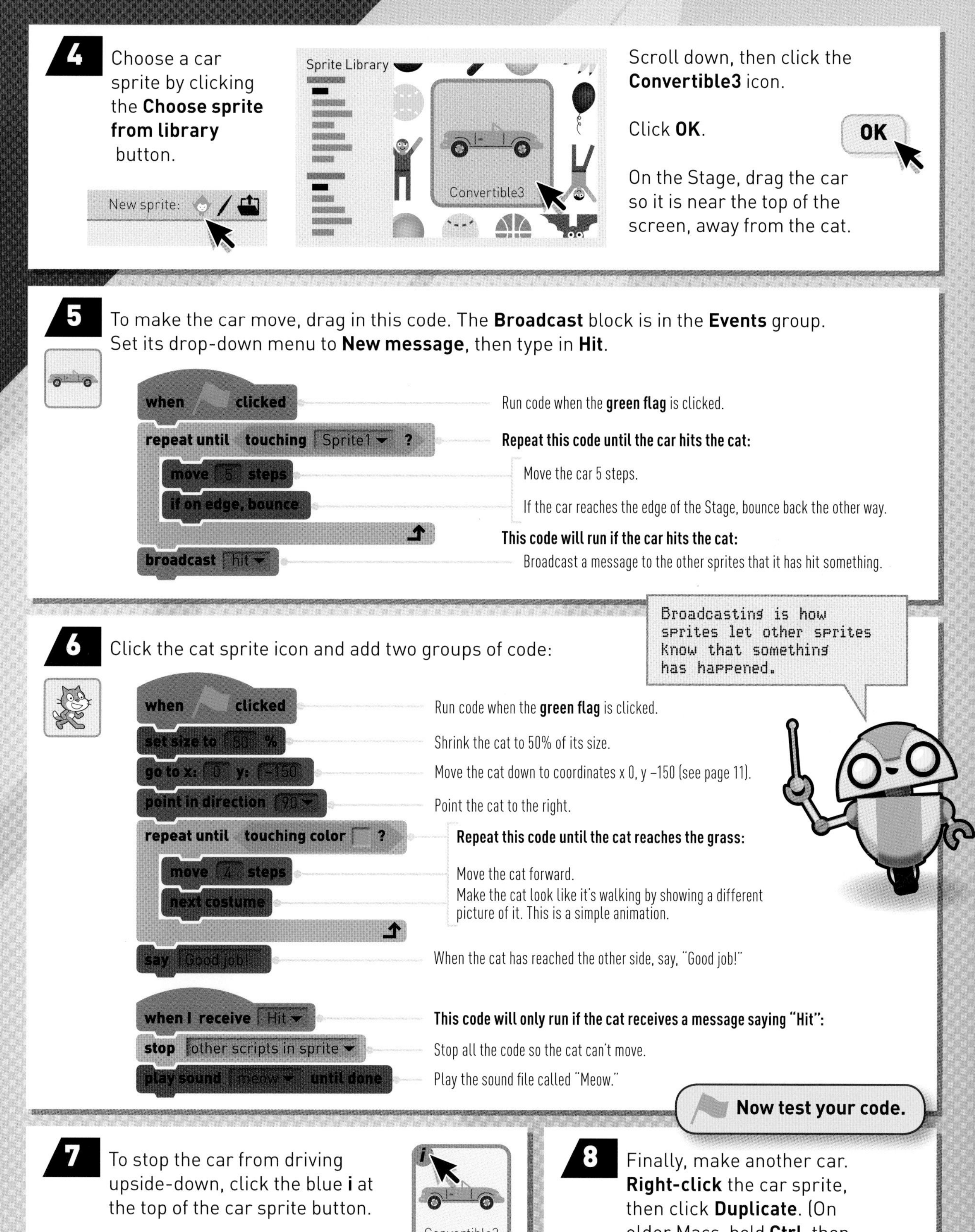

4

Choose a car sprite by clicking the **Choose sprite from library** button.

Scroll down, then click the **Convertible3** icon.

Click **OK**.

On the Stage, drag the car so it is near the top of the screen, away from the cat.

5

To make the car move, drag in this code. The **Broadcast** block is in the **Events** group. Set its drop-down menu to **New message**, then type in **Hit**.

```
when [flag] clicked
repeat until touching [Sprite1 ▾] ?
    move (5) steps
    if on edge, bounce
broadcast [hit ▾]
```

- Run code when the **green flag** is clicked.
- **Repeat this code until the car hits the cat:**
  - Move the car 5 steps.
  - If the car reaches the edge of the Stage, bounce back the other way.
- **This code will run if the car hits the cat:**
  - Broadcast a message to the other sprites that it has hit something.

6

Click the cat sprite icon and add two groups of code:

Broadcasting is how sprites let other sprites know that something has happened.


```
when [flag] clicked
set size to (50) %
go to x: (0) y: (-150)
point in direction (90 ▾)
repeat until touching color [ ] ?
    move (4) steps
    next costume
say [Good job!]
```

- Run code when the **green flag** is clicked.
- Shrink the cat to 50% of its size.
- Move the cat down to coordinates x 0, y –150 (see page 11).
- Point the cat to the right.
- **Repeat this code until the cat reaches the grass:**
  - Move the cat forward.
  - Make the cat look like it's walking by showing a different picture of it. This is a simple animation.
- When the cat has reached the other side, say, "Good job!"

```
when I receive [Hit ▾]
stop [other scripts in sprite ▾]
play sound [meow ▾] until done
```

- **This code will only run if the cat receives a message saying "Hit":**
- Stop all the code so the cat can't move.
- Play the sound file called "Meow."

Now test your code.

7

To stop the car from driving upside-down, click the blue **i** at the top of the car sprite button.

Set the **Rotation style** to left-right. Do the same for the cat.

8

Finally, make another car. **Right-click** the car sprite, then click **Duplicate**. (On older Macs, hold **Ctrl**, then click.) Drag the new car onto the other side of the road.

LEVEL 2 GAMES

Now that you have progressed beyond Level 1, you will find the Level 2 games just a little more challenging to program but more fun to play. We will be adding extra features, such as a scoring system. We will make our games more exciting with random numbers and animations. Here are some quick explanations about the new ideas used in Level 2.

A variable is a little like a special box...

...that has something important stored inside.

VARIABLES: CREATING A SCORE

Computer programs use "variables" as a way to store pieces of data or information. Variables can be used to store things like the score in a game or the speed a sprite is moving. Unlike normal numbers, variables can change their value—so whenever you score a point, the score variable can go up by 1.

How to create a variable:

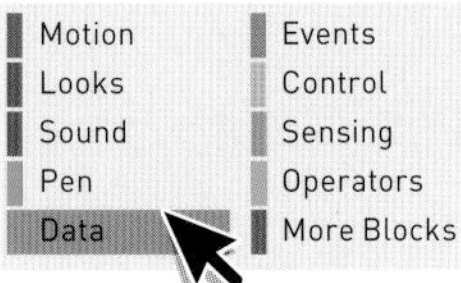

1. Click the **Data** group.

2. Click **Make a variable**.

Variable name: Score

3. Call it **Score**.

OK

4. Then click **OK**.

1. At the start of a game:

set Score ▾ to 0

Put the **Set score to** block near the start of your program to make sure the score is reset to 0 each time you play.

2. Increasing the score:

change Score ▾ by 1

Use the **Change score** code block to make the score variable go up. We need this code to run whenever we score a point.

3. At the end of a game:

In Scratch, variables are normally shown on screen all the time. We can also use a **Say** code block from the **Looks** group to show the score in a speech box at the end of a game.

say Score

Don't type the word "Score"—drag the **Score** block from the **Data** group.

4

You scored 4

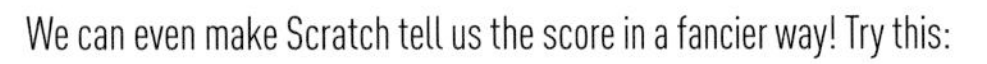

We can even make Scratch tell us the score in a fancier way! Try this:

say

say join You scored world
Score

1. Drag a **Say** block from the **Looks** group.

2. Get a **Join** code block from the **Operators** group. Drag it into the **Say** code block.

3. Type **You scored** in the left hole of the **Join** block.

4. Drag the **Score** block into the right-hand hole.

PICKING RANDOM NUMBERS

It would be boring if games were always the same each time we played them. For example, if we were playing a board game, we might throw a die to choose how far a player moves. We would have no idea which number between 1 and 6 the die would show, because the result is random. In a computer game, we can also get the computer to pick a random number.

This is the lowest number that can be picked.

This is the highest number that can be picked.

Catch the Donut (page 30) uses this code to pick a random place for each donut to fall from. Create this code and click it. Experiment with the two values.

CREATING ANIMATIONS

For *Up in the Clouds* (page 32), we will create our own animation to make it look like a biplane's propeller is rotating. We will create two "costumes" for the plane, one with the propeller up and one with it down. Scratch will switch quickly between the two. Once you have mastered this animation technique, you can create your own animations, from dancing flowers to waving dogs.

1. Draw whatever you want to animate—see page 32 for help drawing a biplane.

2. Next we will create another "costume" to show a slightly different version of the sprite. In the panel down the center of your screen, **right-click Costume1**. (On older Macs, hold **Ctrl**, then click.)

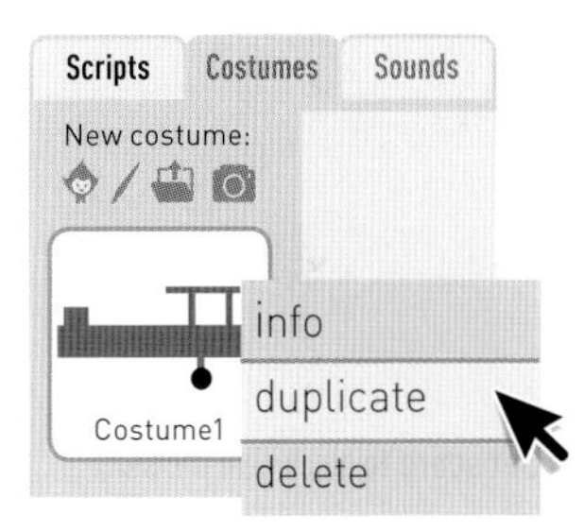

3. Click **Duplicate**. Our plane sprite now has two costumes.

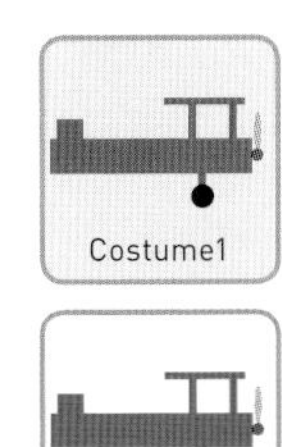

4. Now we make the second costume slightly different. For this example, we will flip the propeller.

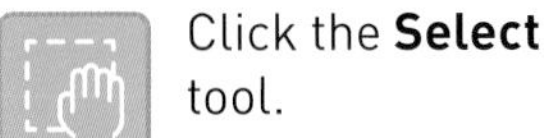

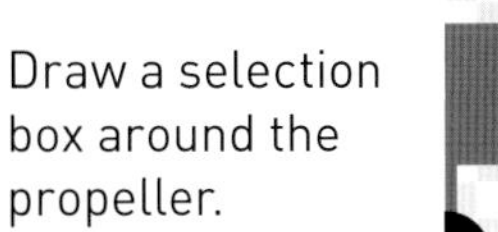

Click the **Select** tool.

Draw a selection box around the propeller.

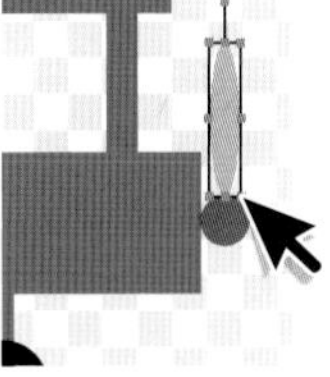

5. Click the **Flip up-down** button. (It's at the top right of the Drawing Area.)

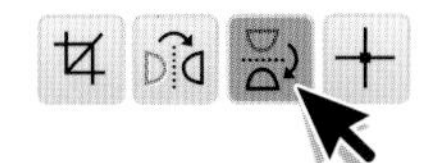

6. Drag down the propeller.

7. Click the **Next costume** code block to switch between the two costumes and see the propeller turn.

DOG AND BONE

Half the fun of a game is seeing your score go up as you play! We are going to create a game that uses a variable (see page 26) to store the number of bones a dog eats. We will also use a simple animation to make the dog look like it is walking.

1 Start a new Scratch file and delete the cat sprite:

In the Sprites Pane, **right-click** the cat sprite icon. (On older Macs, hold **Ctrl**, then click.) Click **Delete**.

2 Choose a dog sprite by clicking the **Choose sprite from library** button.

Scroll down then click the **Dog2** sprite. Click **OK**.

3 Now you need to create a variable so that we can add a score. Turn back to page 26 if you need help.

Choose the **Data** group and click **Make a variable**.

Give your variable a name: **Score**.

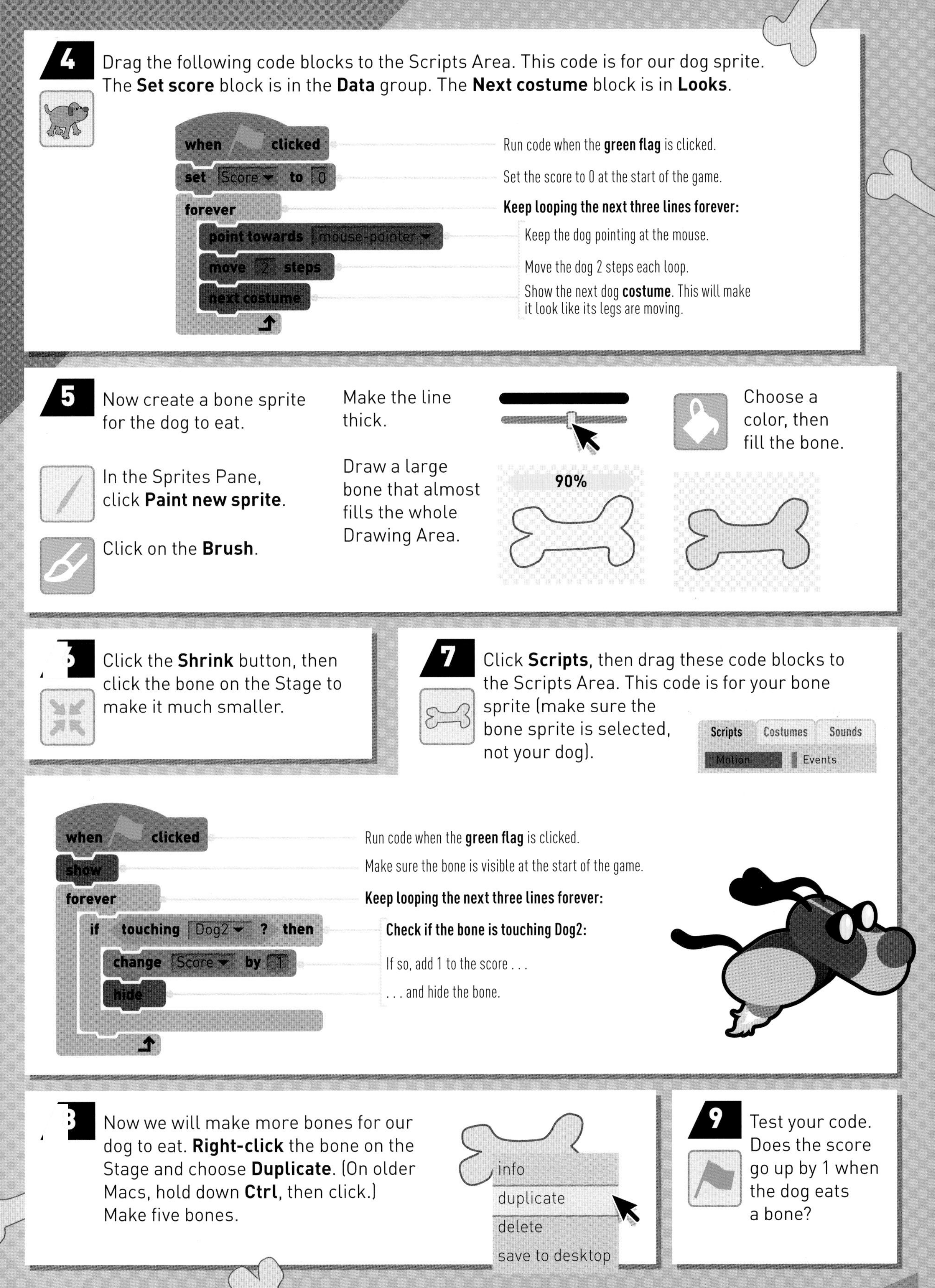

4

Drag the following code blocks to the Scripts Area. This code is for our dog sprite. The **Set score** block is in the **Data** group. The **Next costume** block is in **Looks**.

```
when [flag] clicked
set Score ▾ to 0
forever
    point towards mouse-pointer ▾
    move 2 steps
    next costume
```

- Run code when the **green flag** is clicked.
- Set the score to 0 at the start of the game.
- **Keep looping the next three lines forever:**
  - Keep the dog pointing at the mouse.
  - Move the dog 2 steps each loop.
  - Show the next dog **costume**. This will make it look like its legs are moving.

5

Now create a bone sprite for the dog to eat.

In the Sprites Pane, click **Paint new sprite**.

Click on the **Brush**.

Make the line thick.

Draw a large bone that almost fills the whole Drawing Area.

90%

Choose a color, then fill the bone.

6

Click the **Shrink** button, then click the bone on the Stage to make it much smaller.

7

Click **Scripts**, then drag these code blocks to the Scripts Area. This code is for your bone sprite (make sure the bone sprite is selected, not your dog).

Scripts | Costumes | Sounds

Motion | Events

```
when [flag] clicked
show
forever
    if <touching Dog2 ▾ ?> then
        change Score ▾ by 1
        hide
```

- Run code when the **green flag** is clicked.
- Make sure the bone is visible at the start of the game.
- **Keep looping the next three lines forever:**
  - **Check if the bone is touching Dog2:**
  - If so, add 1 to the score . . .
  - . . . and hide the bone.

8

Now we will make more bones for our dog to eat. **Right-click** the bone on the Stage and choose **Duplicate**. (On older Macs, hold down **Ctrl**, then click.) Make five bones.

info
duplicate
delete
save to desktop

9

Test your code. Does the score go up by 1 when the dog eats a bone?

CATCH THE DONUT

You have probably come across this type of game quite often. The player has to catch the falling donuts. Each caught donut is worth one point—we will store the points in a score variable. We will also use a timer so the player has thirty seconds to catch as many donuts as they can. The time limit will make people eager to play again and beat their best score.

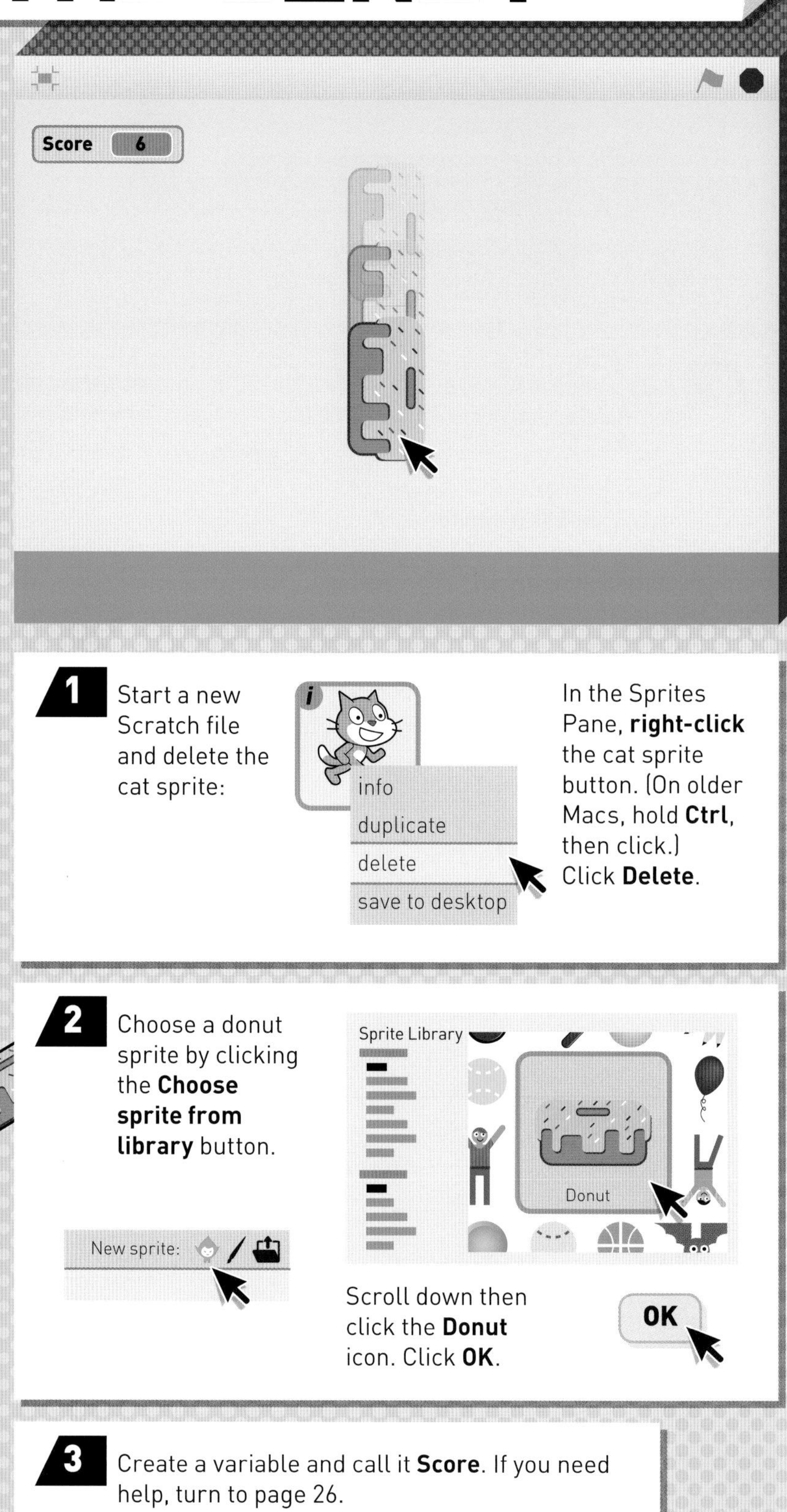

1 Start a new Scratch file and delete the cat sprite:

In the Sprites Pane, **right-click** the cat sprite button. (On older Macs, hold **Ctrl**, then click.) Click **Delete**.

2 Choose a donut sprite by clicking the **Choose sprite from library** button.

Scroll down then click the **Donut** icon. Click **OK**.

3 Create a variable and call it **Score**. If you need help, turn to page 26.

4 Drag the following code blocks onto the Scripts Area. The **Pick random** block is in the **Operators** group (along with the other green blocks). Make sure you drop it in the x coordinate hole.

For help with understanding random numbers, turn to page 27.

```
when [flag] clicked
set [Score ▾] to [0]
reset timer
point in direction [180 ▾]
go to x: (pick random (-200) to (200)) y: (105)
repeat until <(timer) > [30]>
    move (5) steps
    if <touching [edge ▾] ?> then
        go to x: (pick random (-200) to (200)) y: (105)
    end
end
say (join [Out of time! You scored] (Score))
```

Run code when the **green flag** is clicked.

Set the score to 0 at the start of the game.

Reset the timer to 0 seconds at the start of the game.

Point the donut so it falls down the screen.

Start the donut at a random position at the top of the Stage.

Repeat the following commands until 30 seconds are up:

Move the donut 5 steps each loop.

If the donut reaches the edge of the screen:

Move the donut to a random position at the top of the Stage.

This line will run after 30 seconds:
Show a sentence joining "Out of time! You scored" and the **Score** variable.

5 Click the **green flag** to test your code. The donuts should fall from random positions. But we need to make the score go up if we click on a donut. Click **Scripts** then drag these blocks to the Scripts Area:

```
when this sprite clicked
change [Score ▾] by (1)
go to x: (pick random (-200) to (200)) y: (105)
```

Run code when the donut is clicked.

Make the score go up by 1 point.

Move donut to a random position at the top of the Stage.

Does the score go up by 1 point every time you click on a donut? If not, check your code and test it again. Now get a friend to try your game!

EXPERIMENT

What happens if you change the value **30** in this **Repeat until** block? Remember: **>** means "more than."

```
repeat until <(timer) > [30]>
```

Try a different number instead of **5** in this code block. How does this change the game?

```
move (5) steps
```

UP IN THE CLOUDS

In this game, you get to fly a biplane. The plane is controlled by rotating it, in a similar way to the car in *Drive Me Crazy* on page 18. Every time the plane flies through a cloud, the score goes up by one point. But to make the game harder, as the score goes up, the plane gets faster and faster. We will use animation to make the propeller turn.

Score 3

1 Start a new Scratch file. Delete the cat sprite first:

info
duplicate
delete
save to desktop

2 Click **Backdrops** and draw the sky and ground using the **Rectangle** tool.

3 Start the plane by clicking the **Paint new sprite** button.

Choose the **Rectangle** tool.

At the bottom of the screen, click the shaded rectangle. Click red.

Don't draw any clouds yet!

Draw six red rectangles. Make the first one ¾ of the width of the Drawing Area:

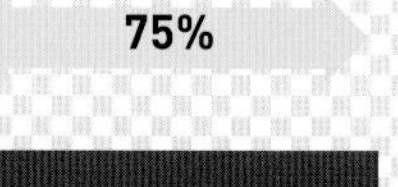

4 Click the **Ellipse** tool. Draw half a propeller and the wheel.

5 Next we will create another **costume** for the biplane to make it look as if the propeller is rotating.

To do this, turn back to page 27 and follow the instructions in the **Creating animations** box.

6 Drag the following code blocks to the Scripts Area. You will need to create a variable called **Score** in the **Data** group. For help with x and y coordinates, or for setting the color in the **Touching color?** block, turn to page 11.

```
when [flag] clicked
set [Score] to [0]
set size to [15] %
point in direction [90]
go to x: [-123] y: [-119]
repeat until <touching color [ ] ?>
    next costume
    move (2 + Score) steps
    if <(x position) > [239]> then
        set x to [-240]
say (join [You scored] (Score))
```

- **when flag clicked** — Run code when the **green flag** is clicked.
- **set Score to 0** — Set score to 0 at the start of the game.
- **set size to 15 %** — Shrink plane to 15%.
- **point in direction 90** — Start with the plane facing right.
- **go to x: -123 y: -119** — Start the plane at the bottom of the screen on the left. (You may need to adjust the y value so the plane never starts on the ground.)
- **repeat until touching color ?** — **Keep running this code until the plane hits the ground:**
  - **next costume** — Show the next costume (the next animation picture).
  - **move 2 + Score steps** — Move the plane 2 steps. As the score goes up, the plane will move faster.
  - **if x position > 239 then** — **If the plane gets to the right of the screen then:**
    - **set x to -240** — Move it back to the left-hand side.
- **say join You scored Score** — **This code runs when the player crashes:** Show a sentence joining "You scored" and the **Score** variable.

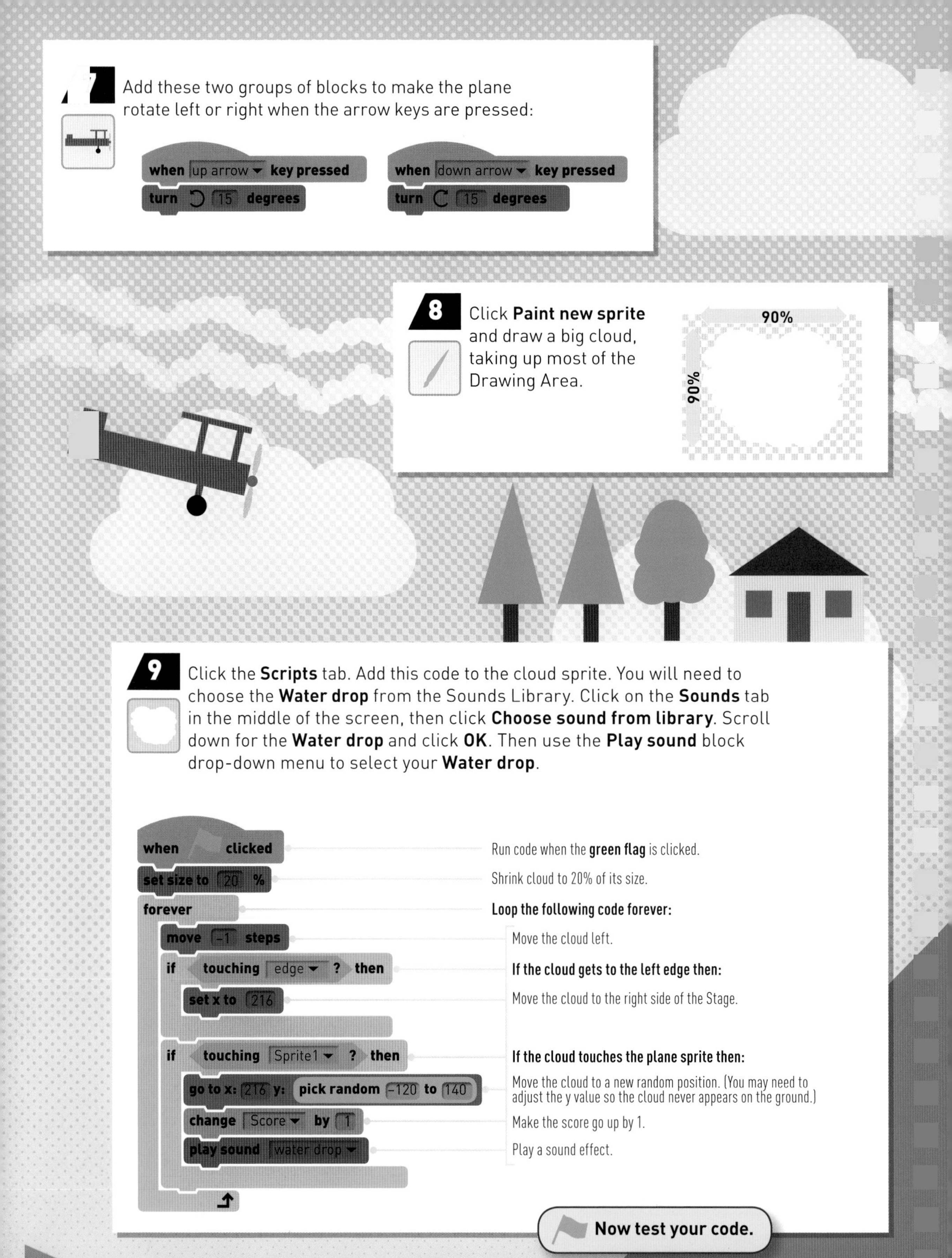

7 Add these two groups of blocks to make the plane rotate left or right when the arrow keys are pressed:

```
when [up arrow v] key pressed
turn ↺ (15) degrees
```

```
when [down arrow v] key pressed
turn ↻ (15) degrees
```

8 Click **Paint new sprite** and draw a big cloud, taking up most of the Drawing Area.

9 Click the **Scripts** tab. Add this code to the cloud sprite. You will need to choose the **Water drop** from the Sounds Library. Click on the **Sounds** tab in the middle of the screen, then click **Choose sound from library**. Scroll down for the **Water drop** and click **OK**. Then use the **Play sound** block drop-down menu to select your **Water drop**.

```
when flag clicked
set size to (20) %
forever
    move (-1) steps
    if <touching [edge v] ?> then
        set x to (216)
    end
    if <touching [Sprite1 v] ?> then
        go to x: (216) y: (pick random (-120) to (140))
        change [Score v] by (1)
        play sound [water drop v]
    end
end
```

- Run code when the **green flag** is clicked.
- Shrink cloud to 20% of its size.
- **Loop the following code forever:**
  - Move the cloud left.
  - **If the cloud gets to the left edge then:**
  - Move the cloud to the right side of the Stage.
  - **If the cloud touches the plane sprite then:**
  - Move the cloud to a new random position. (You may need to adjust the y value so the cloud never appears on the ground.)
  - Make the score go up by 1.
  - Play a sound effect.

Now test your code.

EXPERIMENT

- What happens if you change the number 15 in the **Turn 15 degrees** block (in step 7)? Try small numbers like 1 or 2 and big numbers like 30. Does this make it easier or harder to play the game?

```
when [up arrow] key pressed
turn ↺ (15) degrees
```

```
when [down arrow] key pressed
turn ↻ (15) degrees
```

- Change the number -1 in the **Move -1 steps** in the code that controls the cloud. Try larger or smaller numbers. What happens if the number is positive instead of negative?
- Change the values in the **Pick random -120 to 140** block in step 9. What happens to the cloud?

```
if <touching [Sprite1] ?> then
    go to x: (216) y: (pick random (-120) to (140))
```

CHALLENGES

- Change the scoring system to make the score go up by 10 points every time you hit a cloud.
- Compose a tune for the start of the game, using **Play note** blocks.
- Add trees and buildings to the background to make your game look more exciting.
- Add a timer to your game. Turn to page 31 for hints on how to do this.
- Add an animation to your cloud, so it appears to shrink and grow. Turn back to page 27 for a refresher on how to make animations.
- Try to make the cloud move in a random direction. Hint: In the code shown in step 9, add a **Point in direction** block above the **Change score** block. Use a **Pick random** block to set the angle.
- Design a flying or swimming game of your own. How about making a shark swimming through floating seaweed?

LEVEL 3 GAMES

In this level, we will make our sprites move in more interesting ways, rising and falling as they speed up and slow down. We'll use variables to make that happen. To make our games more sensitive, we will also be doing more complex testing for the position of our sprites.

COMPLEX COLLISION TESTS

We have already used **Touching color?** blocks from the **Sensing** group to test for collisions. In *Snake* (page 44) we need to test to see if the snake has hit its own body. To do this, we could test to see if the snake's head is touching green—the color of its body:

```
repeat until touching color ?
    move 4 steps
```

But if we do that the snake will never move, because the back of its head will always be touching its body. Instead we want to know if its *tongue* is touching its body. To code this, we will check to see if any red on the sprite is touching any green on the Stage:

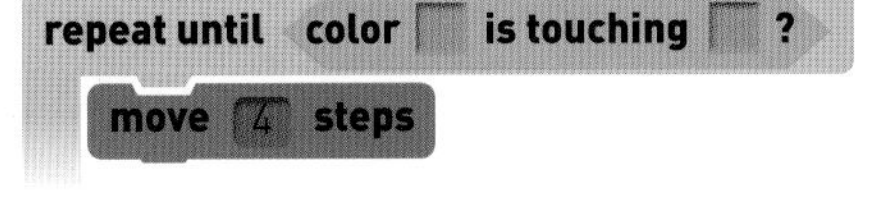

repeat until color is touching ?
move 4 steps

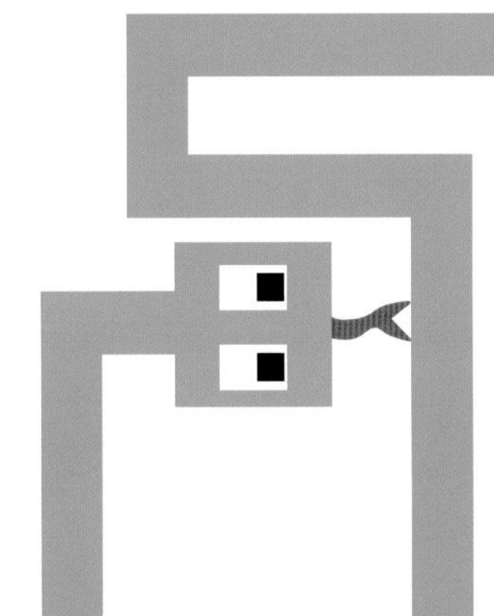

We also need to test to see if the snake has reached the edge of the Stage. To do this we use an **Or** block from the **Operators** group. Our code needs to say: Keep moving until the snake bumps its tail OR hits the edge of the Stage.

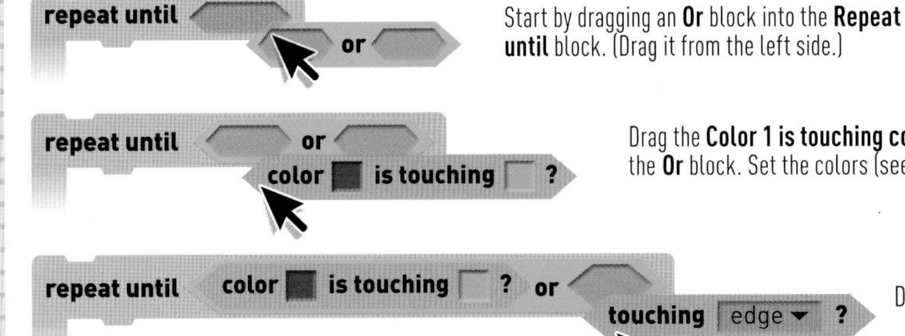

repeat until or
repeat until or
color is touching ?
repeat until color is touching ? or
touching edge ?

Start by dragging an **Or** block into the **Repeat until** block. (Drag it from the left side.)

Drag the **Color 1 is touching color 2?** block into the left hole of the **Or** block. Set the colors (see page 11).

Drag a **Touching edge?** block into the right-hand hole.

TESTING BY LOCATION

In our *Ping Pong* game (page 46), we need to test to see if a point has been scored. To do this, we check where the ball is.

If its x coordinate is greater than 210, it has gone nearly all the way to the right and a point should be given to the red player.

Here's how we build that code:

if then
>

Drag a **Greater than** block from the **Operators** group into an **If then** code block.

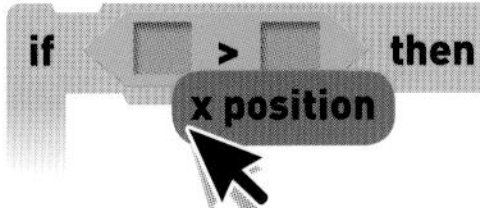

if > then
x position

Drag an **X position** block into the left hole of the **Greater than** block. (It's in the **Movement** group.)

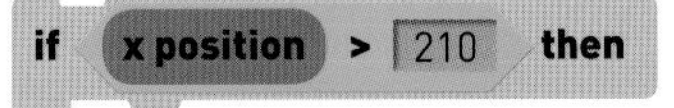

if x position > 210 then

Type "210" in the right hole of the **Greater than** block.

GOING FURTHER WITH VARIABLES

We are now going to use variables (see page 26) to store and change the speed of sprites. This makes their movement look more natural. In *Flappy Fish* (page 38) and *Helicopter Pilot* (page 40) we will use a variable called **Speed** to store the vertical speed of the fish or helicopter—how fast it moves up and down. Positive numbers make it move up, and negative numbers make it move down.

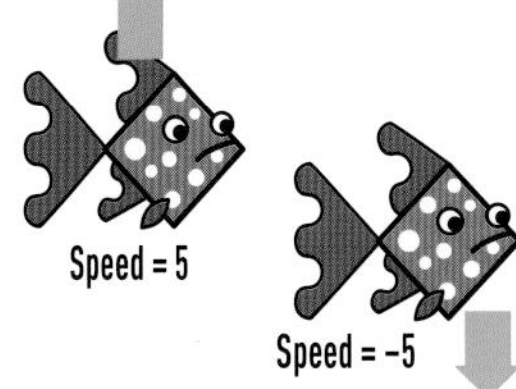
Speed = 5
Speed = –5

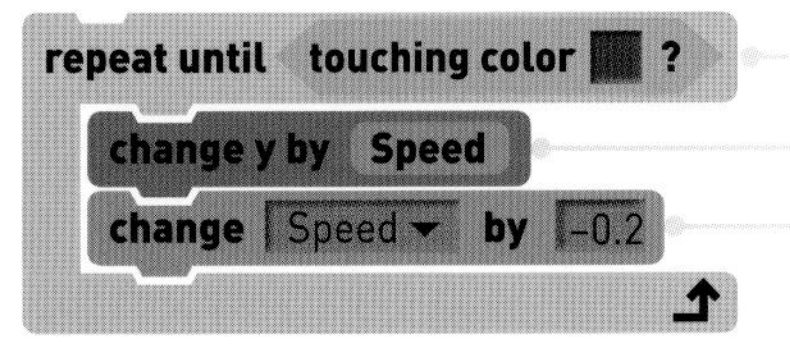
repeat until touching color ?
change y by Speed
change Speed by -0.2

The following lines will loop until the fish touches the pipe (brown):

Move the fish down the screen by the amount stored in **Speed**, so the fish falls as its speed goes down.

Lower the speed so the fish falls down the screen more quickly.

In *Helicopter Pilot* (page 40) we also use the **Speed** variable to change the angle of the helicopter:

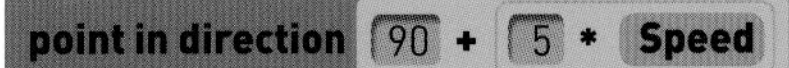
point in direction 90 + 5 * Speed

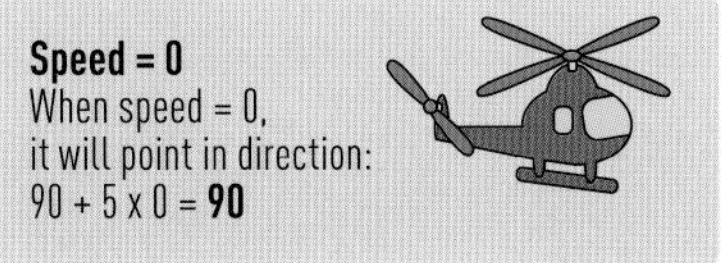

Speed = 0
When speed = 0,
it will point in direction:
90 + 5 x 0 = **90**

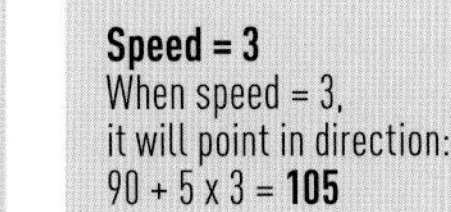

Speed = 3
When speed = 3,
it will point in direction:
90 + 5 x 3 = **105**

Speed = –3
When speed = –3,
it will point in direction:
90 + 5 x –3 = **75**

Let's take a close look at how to make that **Point in direction** code block:

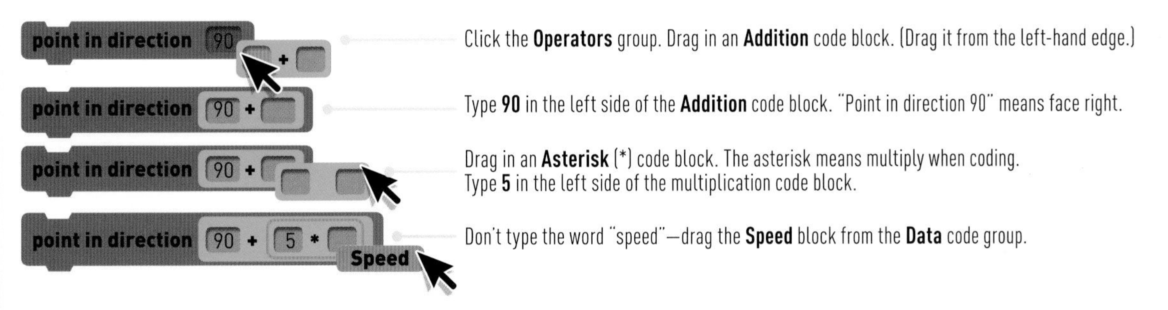
point in direction 90
point in direction 90 +
point in direction 90 +
point in direction 90 + 5 *
Speed

Click the **Operators** group. Drag in an **Addition** code block. (Drag it from the left-hand edge.)

Type **90** in the left side of the **Addition** code block. "Point in direction 90" means face right.

Drag in an **Asterisk** (*) code block. The asterisk means multiply when coding.
Type **5** in the left side of the multiplication code block.

Don't type the word "speed"—drag the **Speed** block from the **Data** code group.

USING VARIABLES WITH SOUND EFFECTS

We can create great sound effects by putting variables into the pitch value of a **Play note** block. As the variable changes, the note played gets higher or lower. Adding sound effects to loops in a sprite's code can slow it down, so in *Helicopter Pilot* (page 40), we add the sound effects to the Stage:

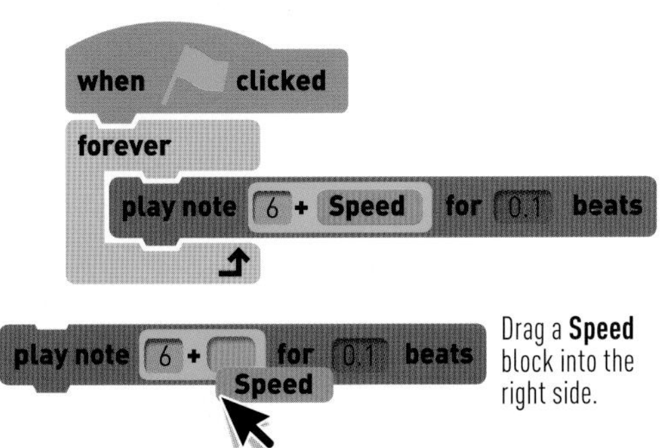
when clicked
forever
play note 6 + Speed for 0.1 beats

To create this effect, drag an **Addition** block into a **Play note** code block.

play note + 0.1 beats

Type "6" in the left hole.

play note 6 + for 0.1 beats
Speed

Drag a **Speed** block into the right side.

FLAPPY FISH

In this game, the player guides a fish to swim between pairs of pipes. It is a side-scrolling game, so we need to program the pipes to move slowly from right to left across the screen. The fish is controlled with a single button, which changes how fast it is falling. The player scores one point for swimming through each pair of pipes.

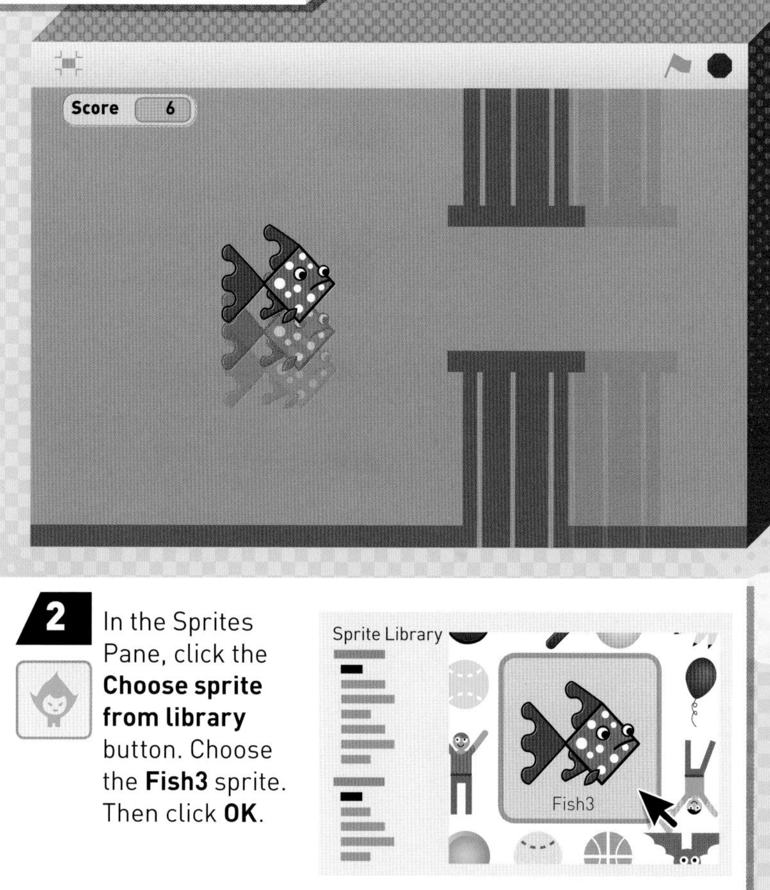

1 Delete the cat sprite first. Click **Backdrops** and draw the sea and ground.

2 In the Sprites Pane, click the **Choose sprite from library** button. Choose the **Fish3** sprite. Then click **OK**.

Sprite Library

Fish3

3 Start the pipes by clicking the **Paint new sprite** button.

Choose the **Rectangle** tool.

At the bottom of the screen, click the shaded rectangle.

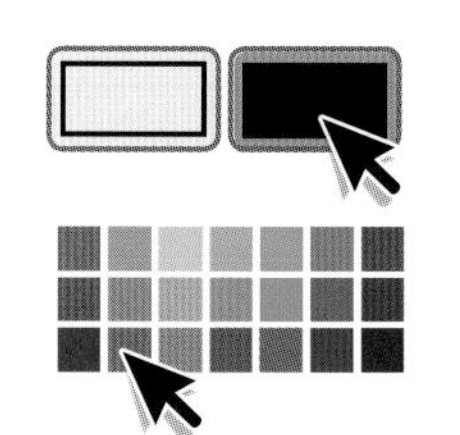

Choose brown.

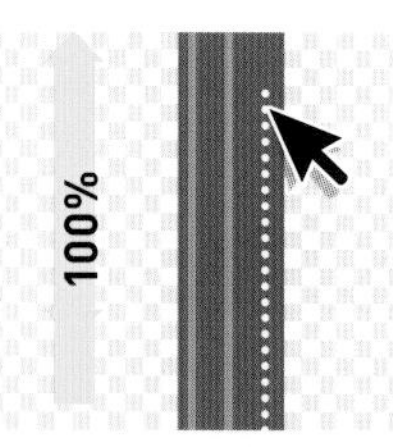

Draw a thin brown pipe from top to bottom of the Drawing Area.

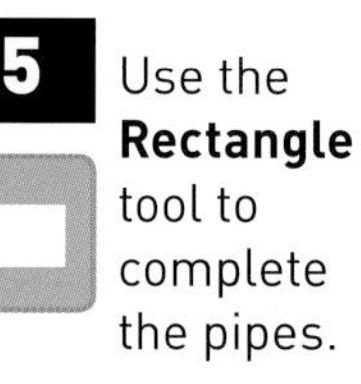

Use the **Line** tool to add some light brown lines.

4 Use the **Select** tool to draw a selection box in the middle of your pipe.

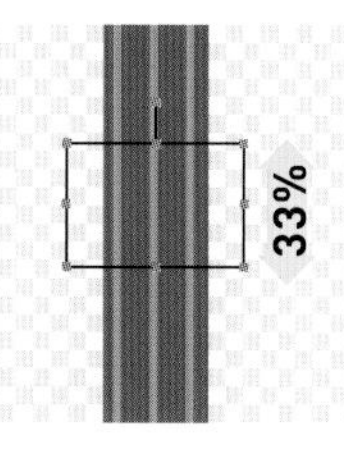

Press the **Delete** key to erase the center. Make sure you leave a big enough gap for your fish to swim through.

5 Use the **Rectangle** tool to complete the pipes.

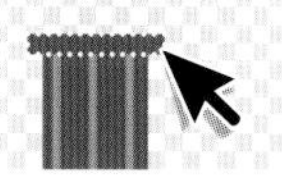

6

Click **Fish3** in the Sprites Pane, then click **Scripts**. Using the **Data** group, create two variables. Call one **Score** and the other **Speed**. For an explanation of how the Speed variable changes the fish's vertical position, turn to page 37.

You will need to choose **Spooky string** from the **Sounds Library** under the **Sounds** tab in the center of the screen. Then use the drop-down menu on the **Play sound until done** block to select it.

Add the following code to make the fish swim down:

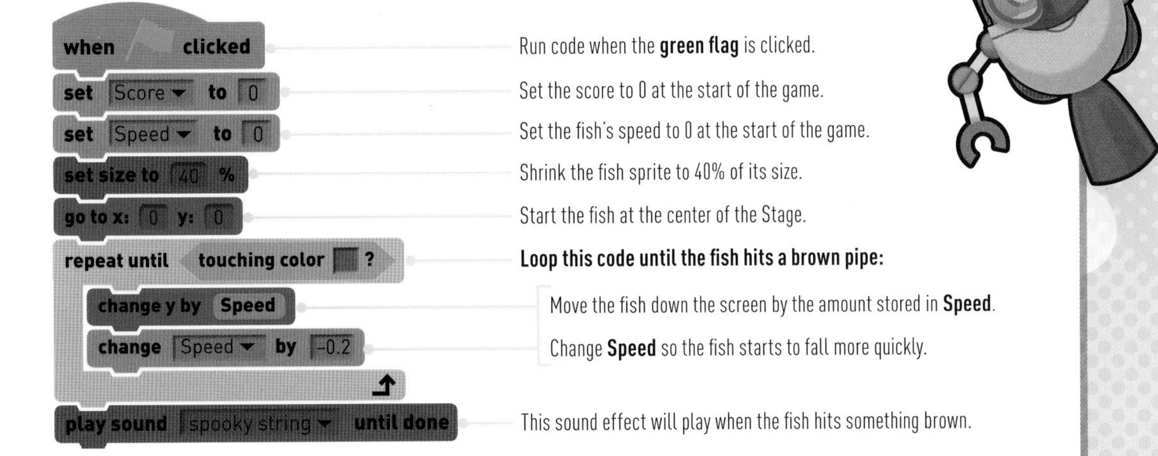
when clicked
Run code when the green flag is clicked.
set Score to 0
Set the score to 0 at the start of the game.
set Speed to 0
Set the fish's speed to 0 at the start of the game.
set size to 40 %
Shrink the fish sprite to 40% of its size.
go to x: 0 y: 0
Start the fish at the center of the Stage.
repeat until touching color ?
Loop this code until the fish hits a brown pipe:
change y by Speed
Move the fish down the screen by the amount stored in Speed.
change Speed by -0.2
Change Speed so the fish starts to fall more quickly.
play sound spooky string until done
This sound effect will play when the fish hits something brown.

7

Now add this code to make the fish swim upward when the player presses the **space bar**.

```
when space key pressed
change Speed by 7
play sound boing
```

When the **space bar** is pressed:
Make the fish's speed go up by 7.
Play a sound effect.

8

Click the pipes in the Sprites Pane. Add the following code to make the pipes scroll across the screen:

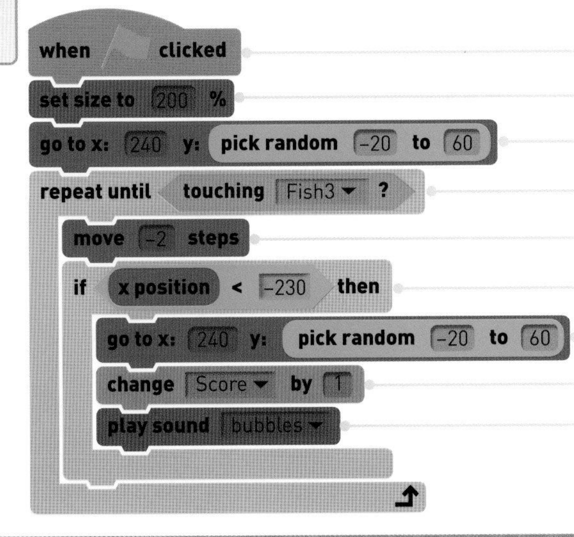
when clicked
set size to 200 %
go to x: 240 y: pick random -20 to 60
repeat until touching Fish3 ?
move -2 steps
if x position < -230 then
go to x: 240 y: pick random -20 to 60
change Score by 1
play sound bubbles

Run code when the **green flag** is clicked.
Make the pipes big so there are no gaps at the top or bottom when we move them up or down.
Start in a random position near the center right of the Stage.
Loop this code until the fish hits the pipes:
Move left 2 steps.
If the pipes get to the left of the Stage then:
Move to a random position near the center right of the Stage.
Increase the score when the fish swims through the pipes.
Play a sound effect.

Now test your code.

HELICOPTER PILOT

This flying game uses some of the same coding techniques as *Flappy Fish* (page 38). The player has to fly a helicopter over skyscrapers. A variable is used to code the helicopter's up and down flight. We'll use a calculation with a variable (see page 37) to create a sound effect that changes with the helicopter's speed.

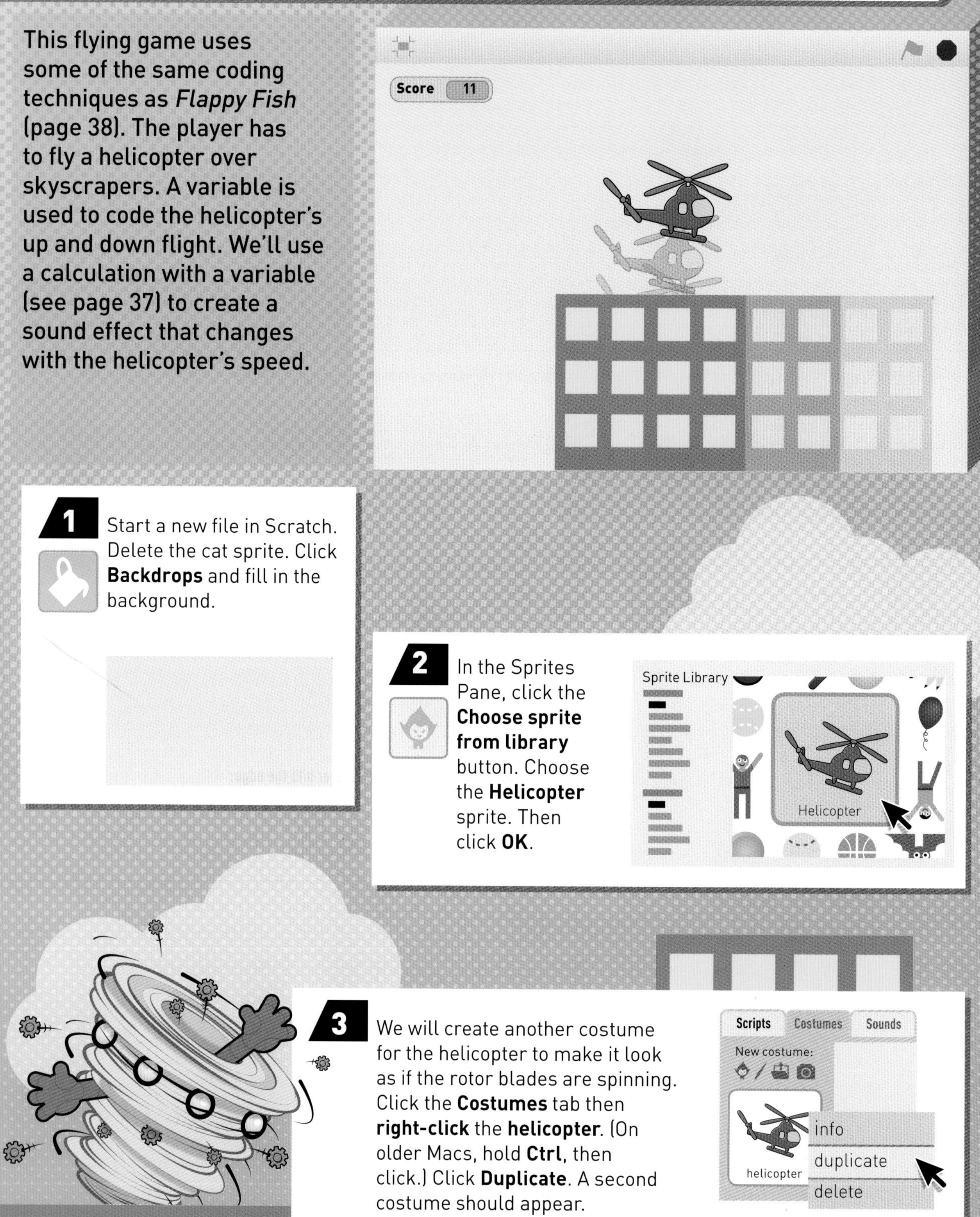

1 Start a new file in Scratch. Delete the cat sprite. Click **Backdrops** and fill in the background.

2 In the Sprites Pane, click the **Choose sprite from library** button. Choose the **Helicopter** sprite. Then click **OK**.

3 We will create another costume for the helicopter to make it look as if the rotor blades are spinning. Click the **Costumes** tab then **right-click** the **helicopter**. (On older Macs, hold **Ctrl**, then click.) Click **Duplicate**. A second costume should appear.

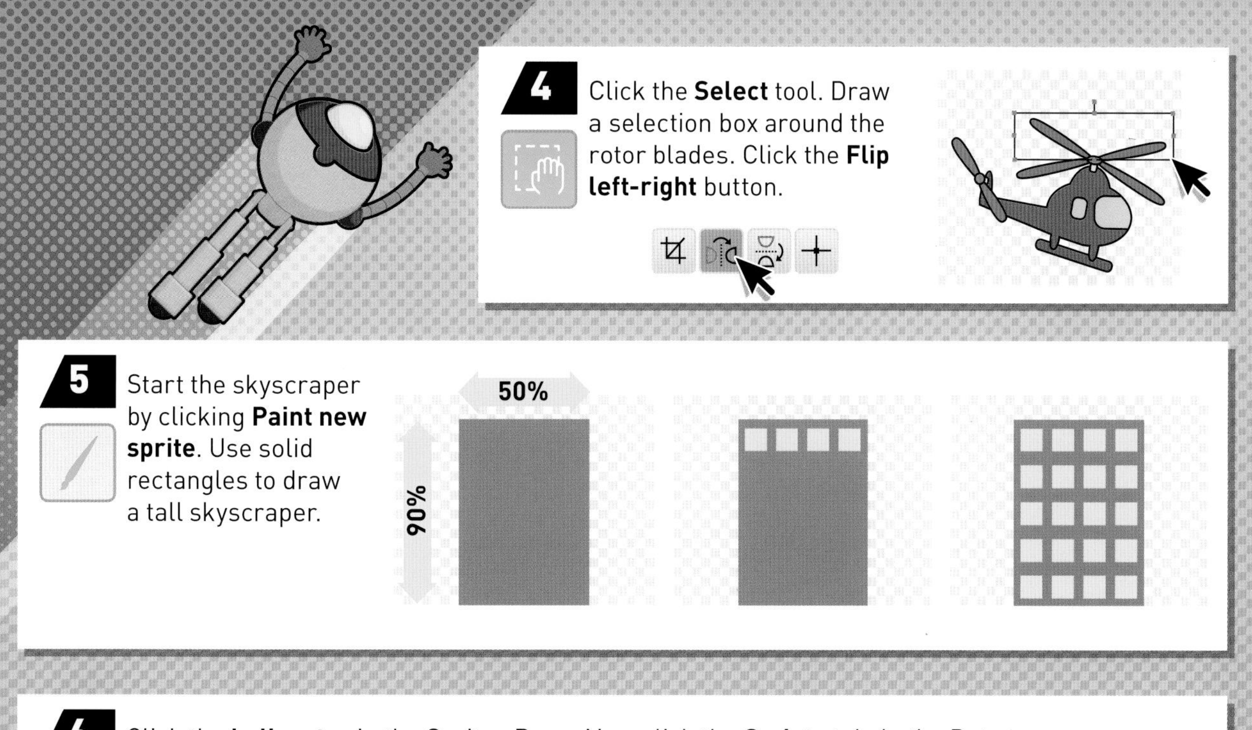

50%
90%

4 Click the **Select** tool. Draw a selection box around the rotor blades. Click the **Flip left-right** button.

5 Start the skyscraper by clicking **Paint new sprite**. Use solid rectangles to draw a tall skyscraper.

6 Click the **helicopter** in the Sprites Pane. Now click the **Scripts** tab. In the **Data** group, create two variables—one called **Score** and the other called **Speed**.

Now create this code. For an explanation of how the **Speed** variable changes the helicopter's flight, turn to page 37.

```
when [flag] clicked
set [Score] to (0)
set size to (50) %
set [Speed] to (0)
go to x: (-50) y: (0)
repeat until <touching [edge] ?>
    next costume
    change [Speed] by (-0.1)
    if <key [up arrow] pressed?> then
        change [Speed] by (0.5)
    point in direction ((90) + ((5) * (Speed)))
    change y by (Speed)
broadcast [Game Over]
```

- Run code when the **green flag** is clicked.
- Set the score to 0 at the start of the game.
- Shrink the helicopter to 50% of its size.
- Set the helicopter's speed to 0 at the start of the game.
- Start the helicopter roughly in the center of the Stage.
- **Loop this code until the helicopter hits the edge:**
  - Make the rotor blade animation work by showing the next costume.
  - Reduce the vertical speed very slightly.
  - **If the Up arrow is pressed:**
  - Increase the vertical speed. By increasing it a small amount, the movement will look smoother.
  - This will make the helicopter point at 90 degrees if the speed is 0. As the value of **Speed** increases, the helicopter will gradually point downward.
  - Move the helicopter up if its speed is high, or down if its speed is a negative number.
- When the helicopter hits the edge, broadcast "Game over" to let the other sprites know they need to stop.

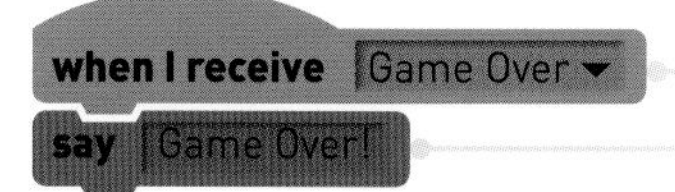

when I receive Game Over
say Game Over!

- If the helicopter hits the skyscraper, it will receive a message, running this code:
- Show a "Game Over!" speech box.

7 Click on the **skyscraper** in the Sprites Pane. Add this code to it:

```
when green flag clicked
go to x: (300) y: (-250)
repeat until <touching [Helicopter v] ?>
    change x by (-3)
    if <(x position) < (-300)> then
        go to x: (300) y: (pick random (-80) to (-280))
        change [Score v] by (1)
    end
end
broadcast [Game Over v]
```

- Run code when the **green flag** is clicked.
- Start the skyscraper on the right, low down.
- **Loop until hit by the helicopter:**
  - Move skyscraper slowly left.
  - **If it has reached the left side:**
  - Move it to the right side, and give it a random y value.
  - Increase the score.
- If the sprites collide, broadcast a message so the helicopter knows it has hit the skyscraper.

Change -300 to -260 or -200 if the skyscraper sticks to the left side of the Stage.

8 In the Sprites Pane, click on the **Stage** and add this code:

```
when green flag clicked
forever
    play note ((6) + (Speed)) for (0.1) beats
end
```

- Run code when the **green flag** is clicked.
- **Loop this code forever:**
  - Play sound effect. Make the sound pitch get higher as the value of **Speed** increases.

```
when I receive [Game Over v]
play sound [snap v] until done
stop [all v]
```

- If the helicopter hits the skyscraper, the skyscraper will broadcast a message, running this code:
- Play sound effect.
- Stop any code running.

Now test your code.

Try adding similar sound effects to the Stage in other games.

EXPERIMENT

- In step 6, alter the value that **Speed** is changed by in the **Change Speed by 0.5** block when the **Up** arrow key is pressed. Try slightly larger or smaller values, such as 0.7 or 0.3.

```
if key up arrow pressed? then
  change Speed by 0.5
```

- Also in step 6, change the number 5 in the **Point in direction 90 + 5 * Speed** block. Try numbers like 3 or 7. Does this make the game look more or less realistic? Does it change how the helicopter moves?

point in direction 90 + 5 * Speed

- Experiment with the values in the sound effects attached to the Stage (step 8). Can you make the pitch of the sound higher or lower? Does this make the game more realistic?

CHALLENGES

- Try to make the rotor blade at the back of the helicopter rotate, too. Hint: Flip the rotor blades in the same way as is shown in step 4.
- Display the score when the game is over.
- Make the skyscraper move faster as the score goes up. Hint: You will need to make changes to the **Change x by -3** block in step 7.
- Compose a tune to play at the beginning of the game and another to play when the helicopter hits the skyscraper.
- Add a timer to your game. Turn to page 31 for hints on how to do this.
- Add an animation to your skyscraper, so the lights in its windows turn on and off as you play.
- Design your own helicopter game. What is the aim of your game? What backdrop will you use? Are there any sprites in the game apart from the helicopter? Will you need to use variables?

SNAKE

The aim of this game is to stop a slithering snake from bumping into itself. To move the snake sprite up, down, left, and right, we use the same ideas as in *Amazing Maze* (page 16). To make the snake's body grow longer and longer, we draw a line on the Stage as it moves around. We then add some code to make sure the snake hasn't hit this line.

Score 338

1 Start a new Scratch file, then delete the cat sprite.

2 To draw the snake's head, start by clicking the **Paint new sprite** button in the Sprites Pane.

Choose the **Rectangle** tool. At the bottom of the screen, click the shaded rectangle.

Choose green.

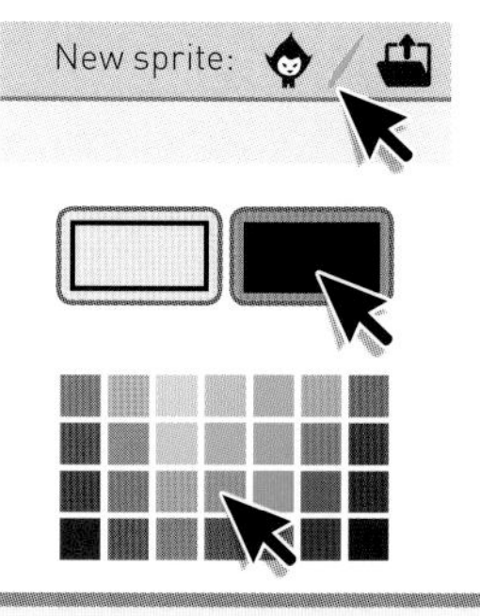

3 Draw the head.

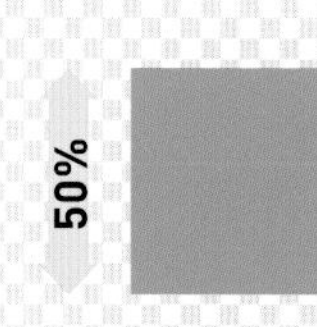

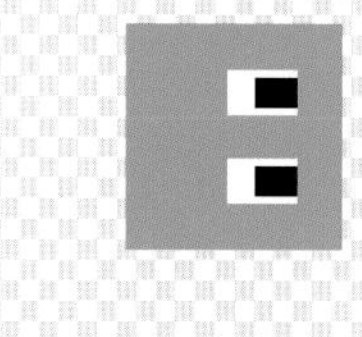

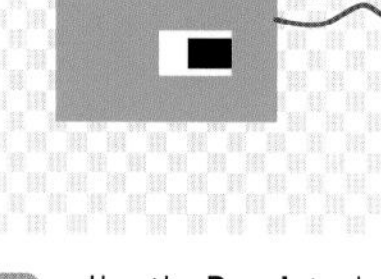

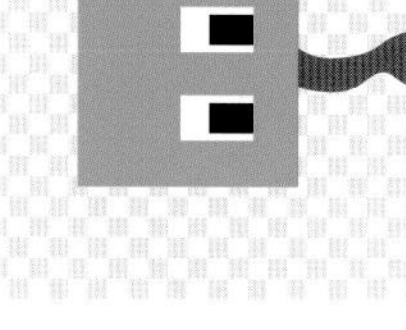

Make a big square about half the height of the Drawing Area. Make sure it is in the center.

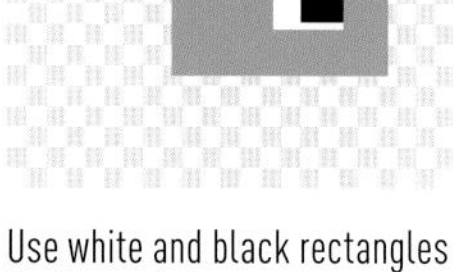

Use white and black rectangles for the snake's eyes.

Use the **Brush** to draw a tongue in red.

Fill the tongue with red.

If you make a mistake use the "Undo" button!

The snake will be drawing a green line—its body—as it moves. In step 4, we will check to see if its red tongue touches this green line.

4 Click the **Scripts** tab and add this code to the snake sprite.

Make sure you add code for each of the four directions.

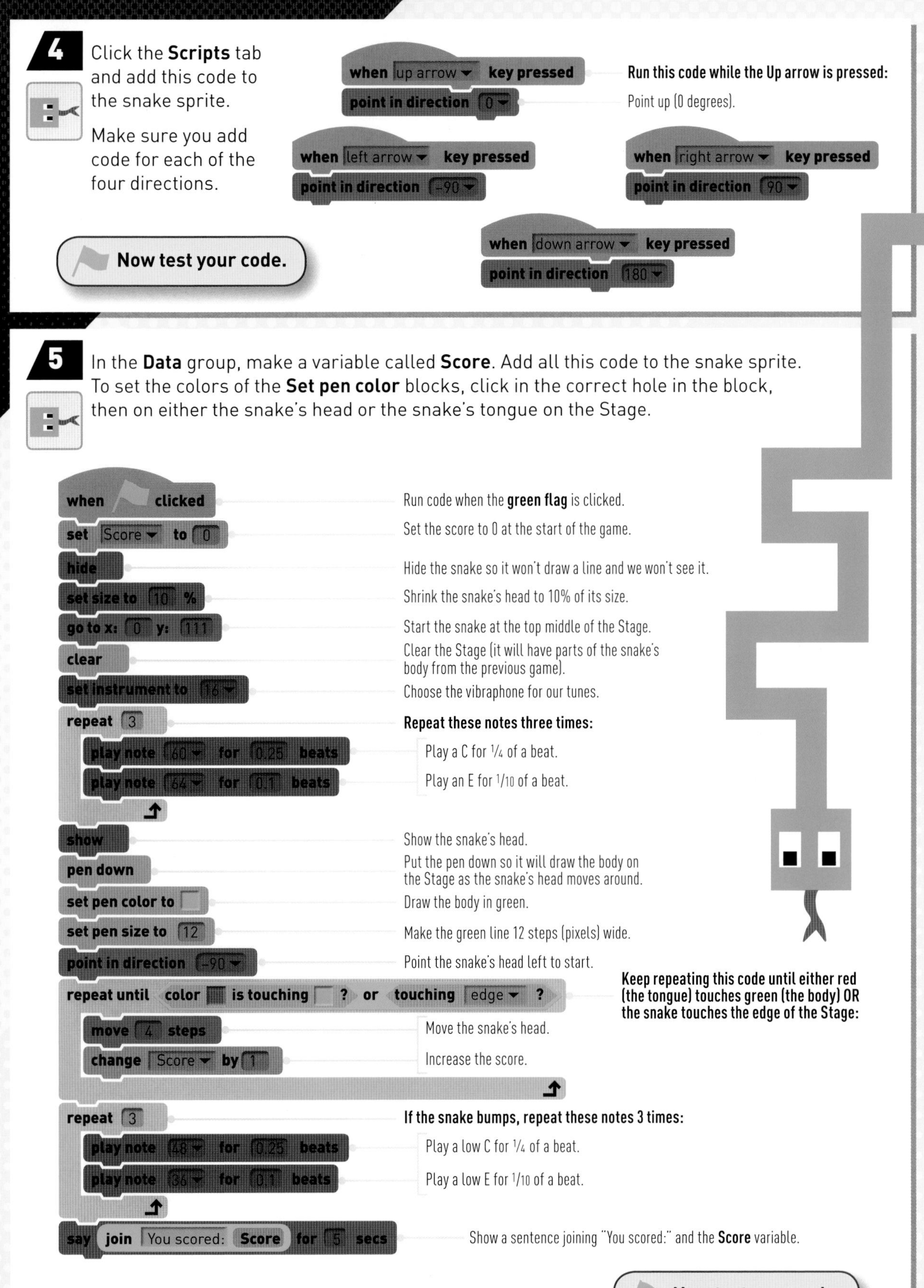

when up arrow key pressed
point in direction 0
Run this code while the Up arrow is pressed:
Point up (0 degrees).
when left arrow key pressed
point in direction -90
when right arrow key pressed
point in direction 90
when down arrow key pressed
point in direction 180
Now test your code.

5 In the **Data** group, make a variable called **Score**. Add all this code to the snake sprite. To set the colors of the **Set pen color** blocks, click in the correct hole in the block, then on either the snake's head or the snake's tongue on the Stage.

when clicked
Run code when the green flag is clicked.
set Score to 0
Set the score to 0 at the start of the game.
hide
Hide the snake so it won't draw a line and we won't see it.
set size to 10 %
Shrink the snake's head to 10% of its size.
go to x: 0 y: 111
Start the snake at the top middle of the Stage.
clear
Clear the Stage (it will have parts of the snake's body from the previous game).
set instrument to 16
Choose the vibraphone for our tunes.
repeat 3
Repeat these notes three times:
play note 60 for 0.25 beats
Play a C for 1/4 of a beat.
play note 64 for 0.1 beats
Play an E for 1/10 of a beat.
show
Show the snake's head.
pen down
Put the pen down so it will draw the body on the Stage as the snake's head moves around.
set pen color to
Draw the body in green.
set pen size to 12
Make the green line 12 steps (pixels) wide.
point in direction -90
Point the snake's head left to start.
repeat until color is touching ? or touching edge ?
Keep repeating this code until either red (the tongue) touches green (the body) OR the snake touches the edge of the Stage:
move 4 steps
Move the snake's head.
change Score by 1
Increase the score.
repeat 3
If the snake bumps, repeat these notes 3 times:
play note 48 for 0.25 beats
Play a low C for 1/4 of a beat.
play note 36 for 0.1 beats
Play a low E for 1/10 of a beat.
say join You scored: Score for 5 secs
Show a sentence joining "You scored:" and the Score variable.
Now test your code.

PING PONG

This game is similar to one of the first ever computer games, called *Pong*. It's a two-player game. One player controls the red bat with the mouse, and the other player controls the blue bat with the arrow keys on the keyboard. Players score points by getting the ball past their opponent.

1 Start a new file in Scratch. **Right-click** the cat. (On older Macs, press **Ctrl**, then click.) Click **Delete**.

2 Click **Backdrops**. Using the **Fill** tool, make a background.

3 Click the **Choose sprite from library** button. Scroll down, then click the **Ball** icon. Click **OK**.

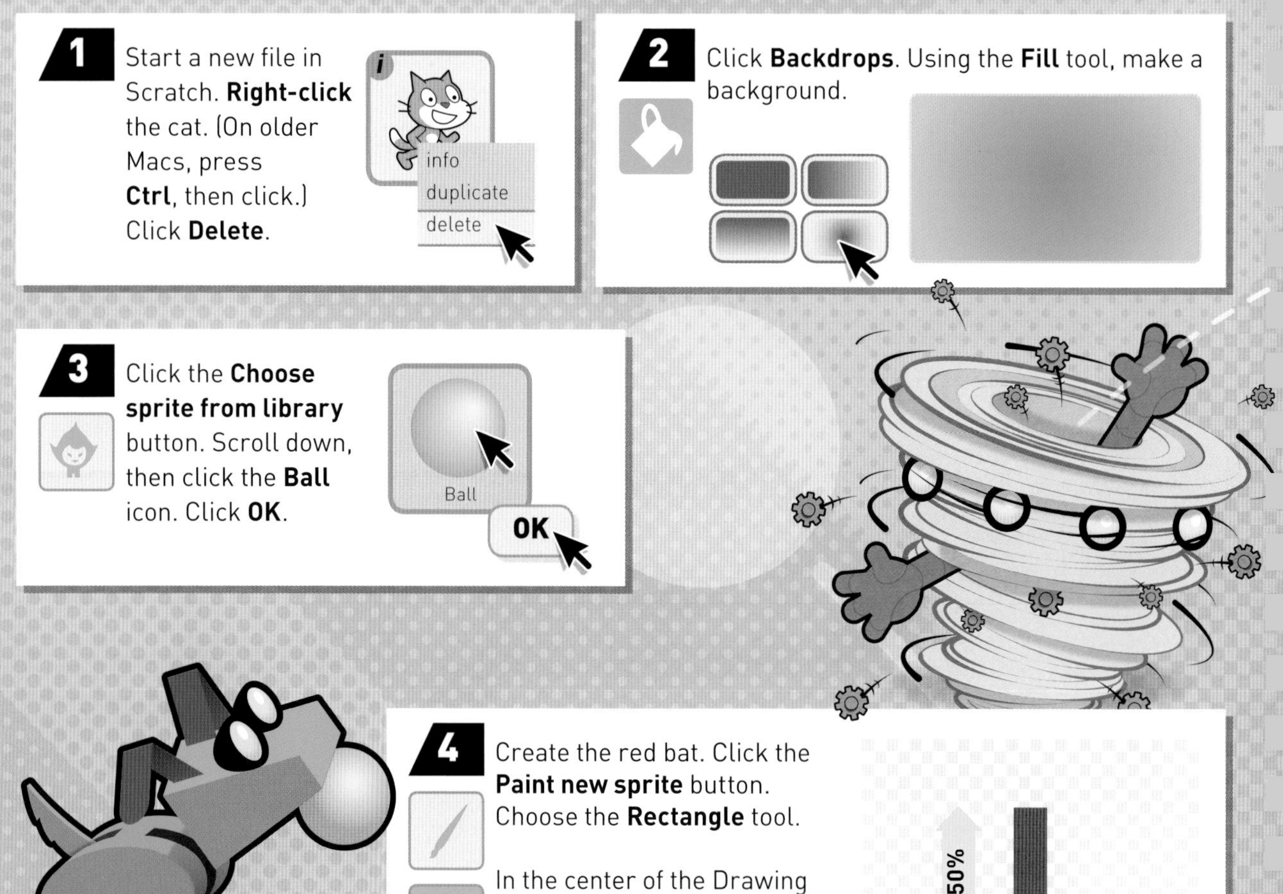

4 Create the red bat. Click the **Paint new sprite** button. Choose the **Rectangle** tool.

In the center of the Drawing Area, draw a tall, solid red rectangle about half the height of the Drawing Area.

50%

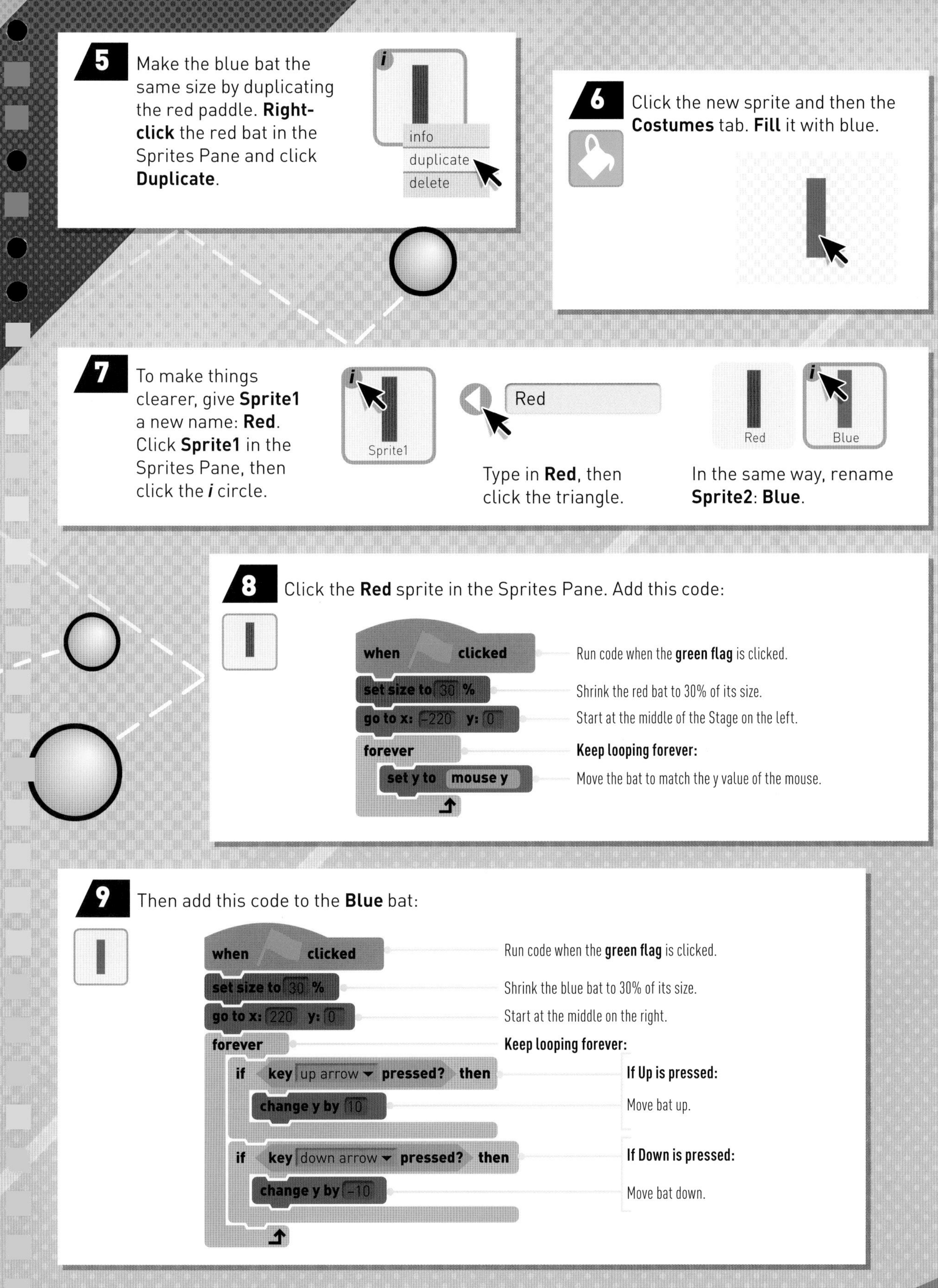

5 Make the blue bat the same size by duplicating the red paddle. **Right-click** the red bat in the Sprites Pane and click **Duplicate**.

info
duplicate
delete

6 Click the new sprite and then the **Costumes** tab. **Fill** it with blue.

7 To make things clearer, give **Sprite1** a new name: **Red**. Click **Sprite1** in the Sprites Pane, then click the ***i*** circle.

Sprite1

Red

Type in **Red**, then click the triangle.

Red Blue

In the same way, rename **Sprite2**: **Blue**.

8 Click the **Red** sprite in the Sprites Pane. Add this code:

```
when [flag] clicked
set size to (30) %
go to x: (-220) y: (0)
forever
    set y to (mouse y)
```

- Run code when the **green flag** is clicked.
- Shrink the red bat to 30% of its size.
- Start at the middle of the Stage on the left.
- **Keep looping forever:**
- Move the bat to match the y value of the mouse.

9 Then add this code to the **Blue** bat:

```
when [flag] clicked
set size to (30) %
go to x: (220) y: (0)
forever
    if <key [up arrow] pressed?> then
        change y by (10)
    if <key [down arrow] pressed?> then
        change y by (-10)
```

- Run code when the **green flag** is clicked.
- Shrink the blue bat to 30% of its size.
- Start at the middle on the right.
- **Keep looping forever:**
- **If Up is pressed:** Move bat up.
- **If Down is pressed:** Move bat down.

10 Click the **Ball** sprite in the Sprites Pane. In the **Data** group, create two variables: **Red** (for the red score) and **Blue** (for the blue score). Then drag over this code:

```
when [green flag] clicked              Run code when the green flag is clicked.
set [Red] to (0)                       Set the red score to 0 at the start of the game.
set [Blue] to (0)                      Set the blue score to 0 at the start of the game.
go to x: (0) y: (0)                    Start the ball in the center of the Stage.
point in direction (-90)               The ball will start by pointing to the left.
forever                                Keep repeating the following code forever:
  if on edge, bounce                   If the ball hits the edge of the Stage, bounce off it.
  move (10) steps                      Move the ball 10 steps in the current direction.
  if <touching [Blue]?> then           If the ball touches the blue bat:
    point in direction (pick random (-70) to (-110))
                                       Point roughly to the left, at a random angle between -70 and -110 degrees.
    play sound [pop]                   Play a sound effect.
  if <touching [Red]?> then            If the ball touches the red bat:
    point in direction (pick random (70) to (110))
                                       Point roughly to the right, at a random angle between 70 and 110 degrees.
    play sound [pop]                   Play a sound effect.
  if <(x position) > (210)> then       If the x coordinate of the ball is greater than 210 (near the right edge of the Stage):
    change [Red] by (1)                Make the red score go up by 1.
    play sound [chord2] until done     Play a sound effect.
    go to x: (0) y: (0)                Move the ball to the center of the Stage.
    point in direction (-90)           Point the ball to the left.
  if <(x position) < (-210)> then      If the x coordinate of the ball is less than -210 (the left side of the Stage):
    change [Blue] by (1)               Make the blue score go up by 1.
    play sound [chord2] until done     Play a sound effect.
    go to x: (0) y: (0)                Move the ball to the center of the Stage.
    point in direction (90)            Point the ball to the right.
```

When making the sound effects blocks, choose your effects from the Sounds Library.

11 Now click the **green flag** to test your code. If it works, get a friend to play with you!

CHALLENGES

- Make the game start with the ball pointing toward the right (blue) bat rather than toward the left.
- Make the ball move in a random direction when the game starts.
- Create a sound effect that plays when the ball bounces off the edge of the Stage.
- Change the scoring system so each player gets 10 points for getting the ball past their opponent.
- Compose a tune that will play if the red player's score reaches 50. Compose a different tune that will play if the blue player's score reaches 50.
- If either player's score reaches 100, stop the game and flash up a message that says, "Game over!"
- Make the ball move in a random direction if it hits a bat.

EXPERIMENT

- Change the code that controls the ball movement (step 10). Experiment with the number 10 in the **Move 10 steps** block.

```
if on edge, bounce
move (10) steps
```

- Alter the values that y is changed by when the arrow keys are pressed to control the blue bat (see step 9). Does this make it harder or easier to play?

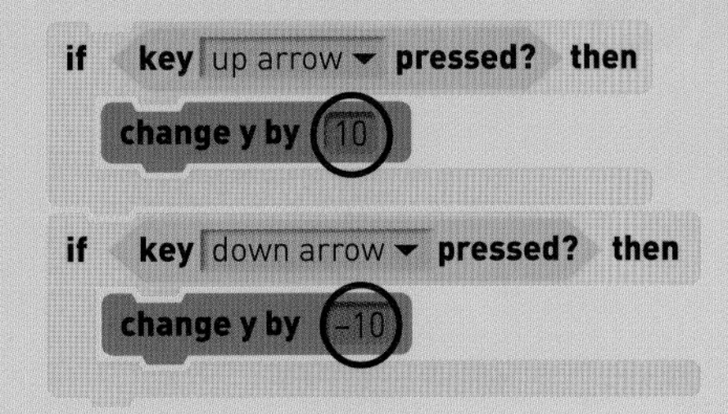
if key up arrow pressed? then
change y by 10
if key down arrow pressed? then
change y by -10

- Change the sizes of the bats from 30% to a slightly larger or smaller value. You could also add code to make the bats smaller (or larger) as the players' points go up. Do these changes make the game harder or easier to play?

LEVEL 4
GAMES

The Level 4 games introduce a useful idea called cloning. So far, you have learned to create extra copies of a sprite by duplicating it with the right-click menu (or holding Ctrl when you click, if you use a Mac). There is a more efficient way of copying sprites: by using code. Scratch calls this cloning. Sprites can be cloned multiple times using loops.

HOW TO CLONE A CAT

Let's start off by cloning the cat sprite. Drag a **Create clone** code block from the **Control** group onto the Scripts Area and click it.

It looks as if nothing has happened. That's because the cloned cat sprite is in the same place as the original cat. Cloning has copied everything about the first cat: its size, any code, and even its location.

If you try dragging the cat sprite, you will see there is a second one behind it.

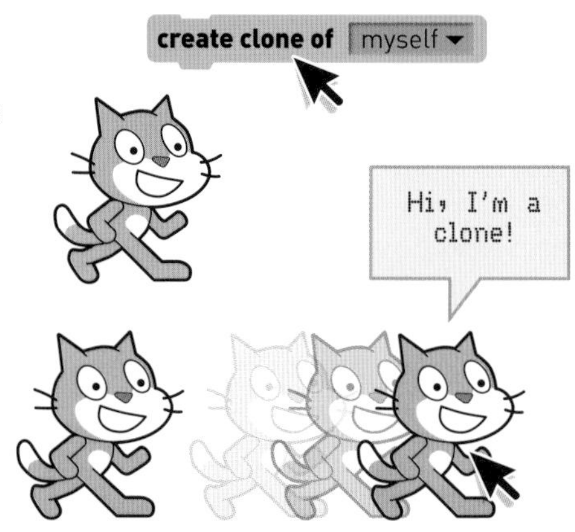
create clone of myself
Hi, I'm a clone!

LOTS OF CATS

We can use loops to make lots of clones quickly. Build the code on the right, then click it.

```
repeat 4
    create clone of myself
```

As before, all the clones are in the same place, so you will have to drag them to see them all.

There is a much better way to create clones, where each clone gets moved to a new random place. Build this code to try it out:

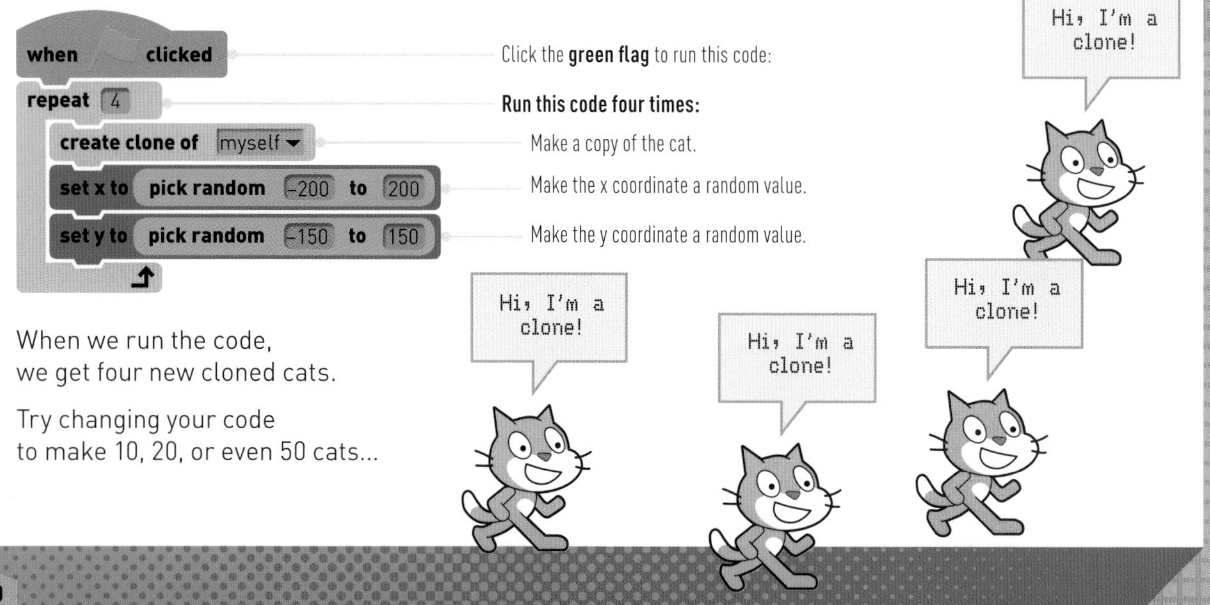
when clicked
repeat 4
create clone of myself
set x to pick random -200 to 200
set y to pick random -150 to 150
Click the green flag to run this code:
Run this code four times:
Make a copy of the cat.
Make the x coordinate a random value.
Make the y coordinate a random value.
Hi, I'm a clone!
Hi, I'm a clone!
Hi, I'm a clone!
Hi, I'm a clone!

When we run the code, we get four new cloned cats.

Try changing your code to make 10, 20, or even 50 cats...

MOVING CLONES

To do more with your clones, it's a good idea to use two different groups of code to separate how the clones are created from how they behave.

To understand this, try creating these two blocks of code on the Scripts Area:

```
when [flag] clicked
hide
repeat (3)
    create clone of [myself v]
```

This piece of code hides the original cat, then creates three clones.

```
when I start as a clone
show
set x to (-250)
set y to (pick random (-150) to (150))
forever
    move (1) steps
```

- when I start as a clone — When each clone starts up, run this code:
- show — Make the clone visible.
- set x to (-250) — Move the clone to the left.
- set y to (pick random (-150) to (150)) — Give it a random y position.
- forever — **Loop forever:**
  - move (1) steps — Move the clone to the right.

Hi, I'm a clone!

THE SAME BUT DIFFERENT

In the *Cat and Mouse* game (page 52), we need four cloned cats. However, we want each cat to move at a different random speed. To do this, we will create a variable called **Speed** in the **Data** group.

To ensure that each **Speed** variable only works with its own cloned sprite, choose the option that says **For this sprite only** when you create it.

New Variable

Variable name: Speed

For all sprites ● For this sprite only

OK Cancel

Change the second part of the program above (under **Moving clones**) to say:

```
when I start as a clone
show
set [Speed v] to (pick random (1) to (10))
set x to (-250)
set y to (pick random (-150) to (150))
forever
    move (Speed) steps
```

- when I start as a clone — Run this code when each clone is made.
- show — Make the clone visible.
- set [Speed v] to (pick random (1) to (10)) — Set the clone's speed to a random value.
- set x to (-250) — Start the clone on the left.
- set y to (pick random (-150) to (150)) — Give it a random y position.
- forever — **Loop forever:**
  - move (Speed) steps — Move the clone right according to the speed it has been set. Each clone has its own speed.

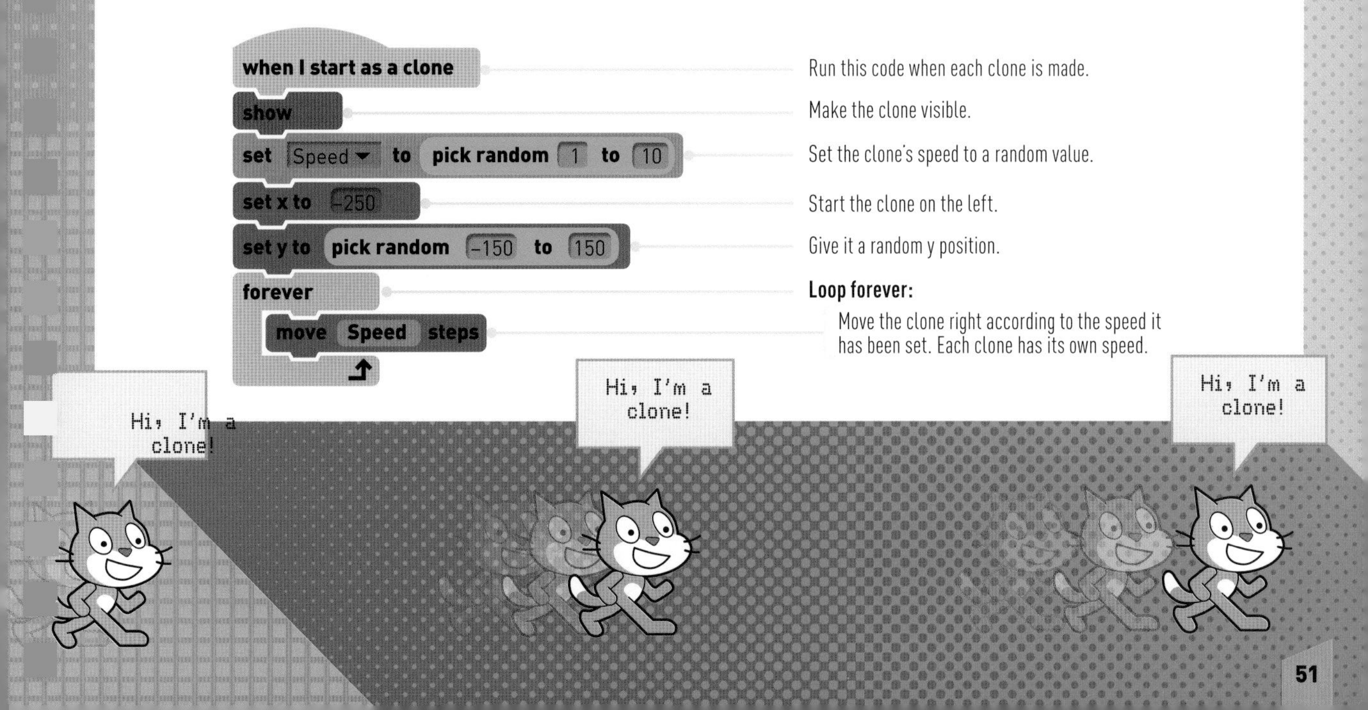

Hi, I'm a clone!
Hi, I'm a clone!
Hi, I'm a clone!

CAT AND MOUSE

For this game, we will be cloning cats—mice beware! If you have never done any cloning before, turn back to page 50 for a quick explanation. Each cat clone is going to appear in a random location and move at a random speed. Of course, the object of the game is for the mouse to escape the cats!

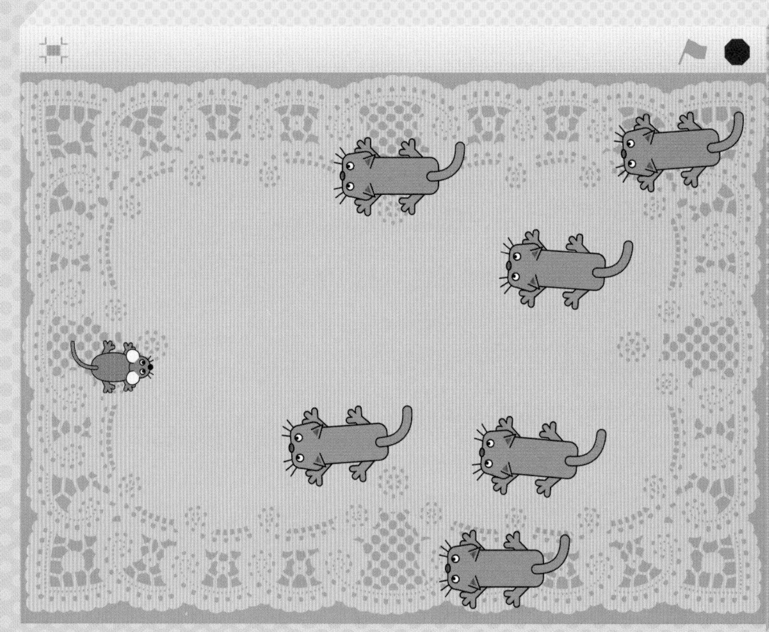

1 Start a new Scratch file, then delete the standard cat sprite. Click **Choose sprite from library** and choose **Cat2**. Click **OK**. Your Sprites Pane should look like this:

2 Now we need to clone the cat. Drag this code to the Scripts Area:

```
when [green flag] clicked          Run code when the green flag is clicked.
point in direction (-90 ▾)         Make the cat sprite face left.
show                               Make sure it is visible.
set size to (60) %                 Shrink it to 60% of its size.
repeat (4)                         Repeat four times (to make four clones):
    create clone of (myself ▾)         Clone a copy of the original cat.
end
hide                               Finally, hide the original cat—its job is done!
```

3 Click the **green flag** to test your code. You won't see all the cats as they will be piled on top of each other! Drag away the top cat—you will find the others underneath.

EXPERIMENT

Before you move to step 4, try changing the number of times the repeat loop runs. What happens?

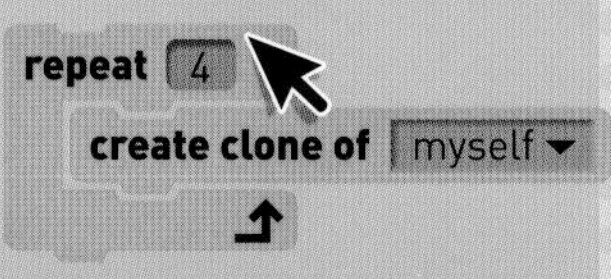

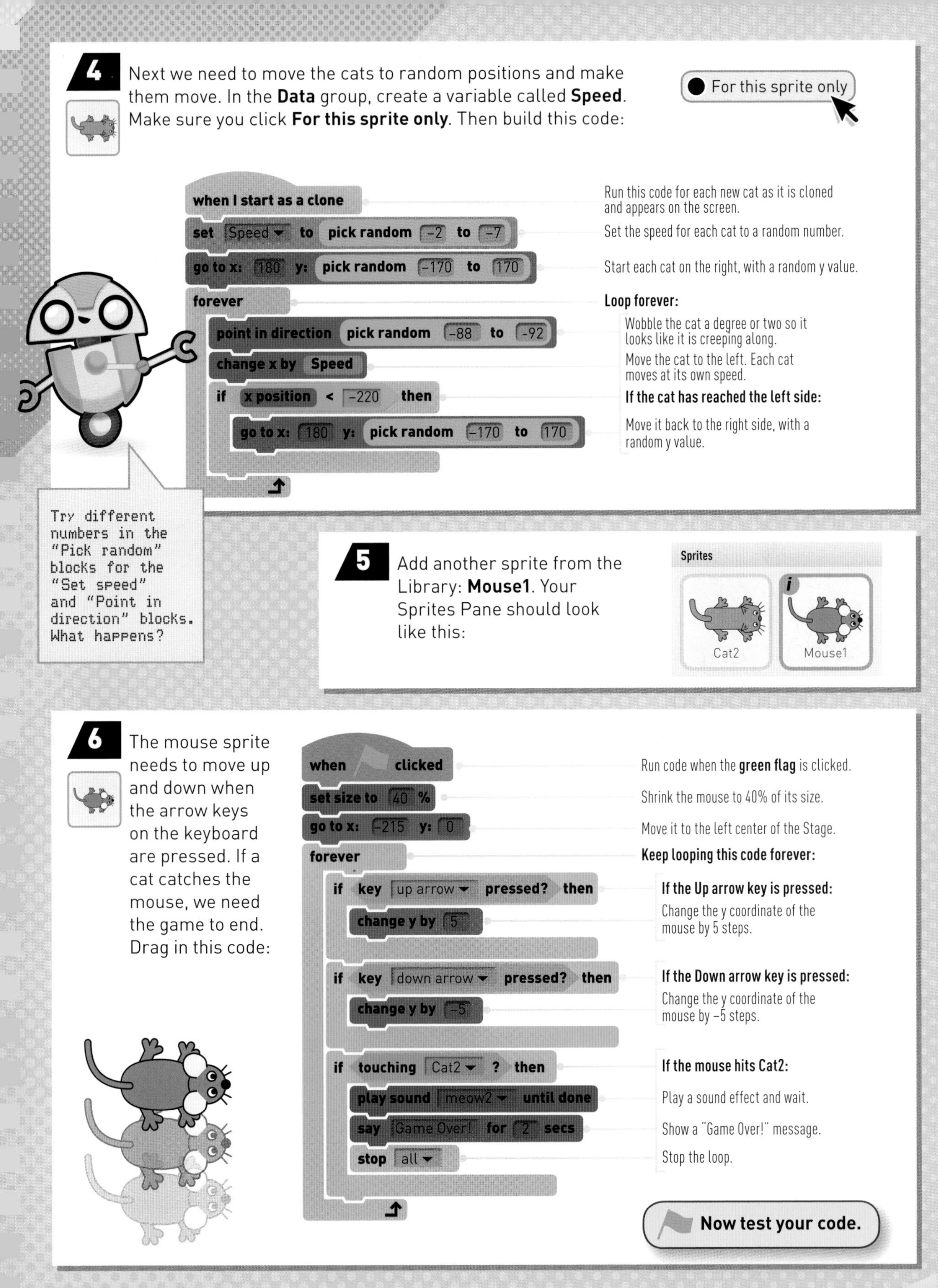

4

Next we need to move the cats to random positions and make them move. In the **Data** group, create a variable called **Speed**. Make sure you click **For this sprite only**. Then build this code:


```
when I start as a clone
set Speed to pick random -2 to -7
go to x: 180 y: pick random -170 to 170
forever
    point in direction pick random -88 to -92
    change x by Speed
    if x position < -220 then
        go to x: 180 y: pick random -170 to 170
```

- Run this code for each new cat as it is cloned and appears on the screen.
- Set the speed for each cat to a random number.
- Start each cat on the right, with a random y value.
- **Loop forever:**
  - Wobble the cat a degree or two so it looks like it is creeping along.
  - Move the cat to the left. Each cat moves at its own speed.
  - **If the cat has reached the left side:**
    - Move it back to the right side, with a random y value.

Try different numbers in the "Pick random" blocks for the "Set speed" and "Point in direction" blocks. What happens?

5

Add another sprite from the Library: **Mouse1**. Your Sprites Pane should look like this:

6

The mouse sprite needs to move up and down when the arrow keys on the keyboard are pressed. If a cat catches the mouse, we need the game to end. Drag in this code:

```
when [green flag] clicked
set size to 40 %
go to x: -215 y: 0
forever
    if key up arrow pressed? then
        change y by 5
    if key down arrow pressed? then
        change y by -5
    if touching Cat2 ? then
        play sound meow2 until done
        say Game Over! for 2 secs
        stop all
```

- Run code when the **green flag** is clicked.
- Shrink the mouse to 40% of its size.
- Move it to the left center of the Stage.
- **Keep looping this code forever:**
  - **If the Up arrow key is pressed:** Change the y coordinate of the mouse by 5 steps.
  - **If the Down arrow key is pressed:** Change the y coordinate of the mouse by –5 steps.
  - **If the mouse hits Cat2:**
    - Play a sound effect and wait.
    - Show a "Game Over!" message.
    - Stop the loop.

Now test your code.

CATCH THE PIZZAS

We are going to use cloning to make lots of pizza sprites fall from a building. Our cat sprite has to catch them! We will give our cat three chances (or three "lives") to catch pizzas. When our cat has lost all three lives, the game is over. We will store this information in a variable called Lives.

Score 12

Lives 1

1 Click the **Stage** icon.

Click **Backdrops**.

Click **Choose backdrop from library**.

Choose **brick wall1**. Then click **OK**.

brick wall1

2 Create the pizza sprite by clicking the **Paint new sprite** button.

New sprite:

Choose the **Ellipse** tool. Click the solid ellipse. Pick a color for dough.

90%

Draw a large circle for the base.

Add red sauce.

Add cheese.

And some olives.

3 Click the **Scripts** tab and add this code to the pizza:

```
when [green flag] clicked
set size to (15) %
point in direction (180 ▾)
repeat (5)
    create clone of [myself ▾]
end
hide
```

- when green flag clicked: Run code when the **green flag** is clicked.
- set size to 15 %: Shrink the pizza to 15% of its size.
- point in direction 180: Point the pizza down—so it falls down the screen.
- **Use a repeat loop to make five pizza clones:**
  - Each loop makes a new cloned pizza.
- hide: Hide the original pizza—we don't need it now.

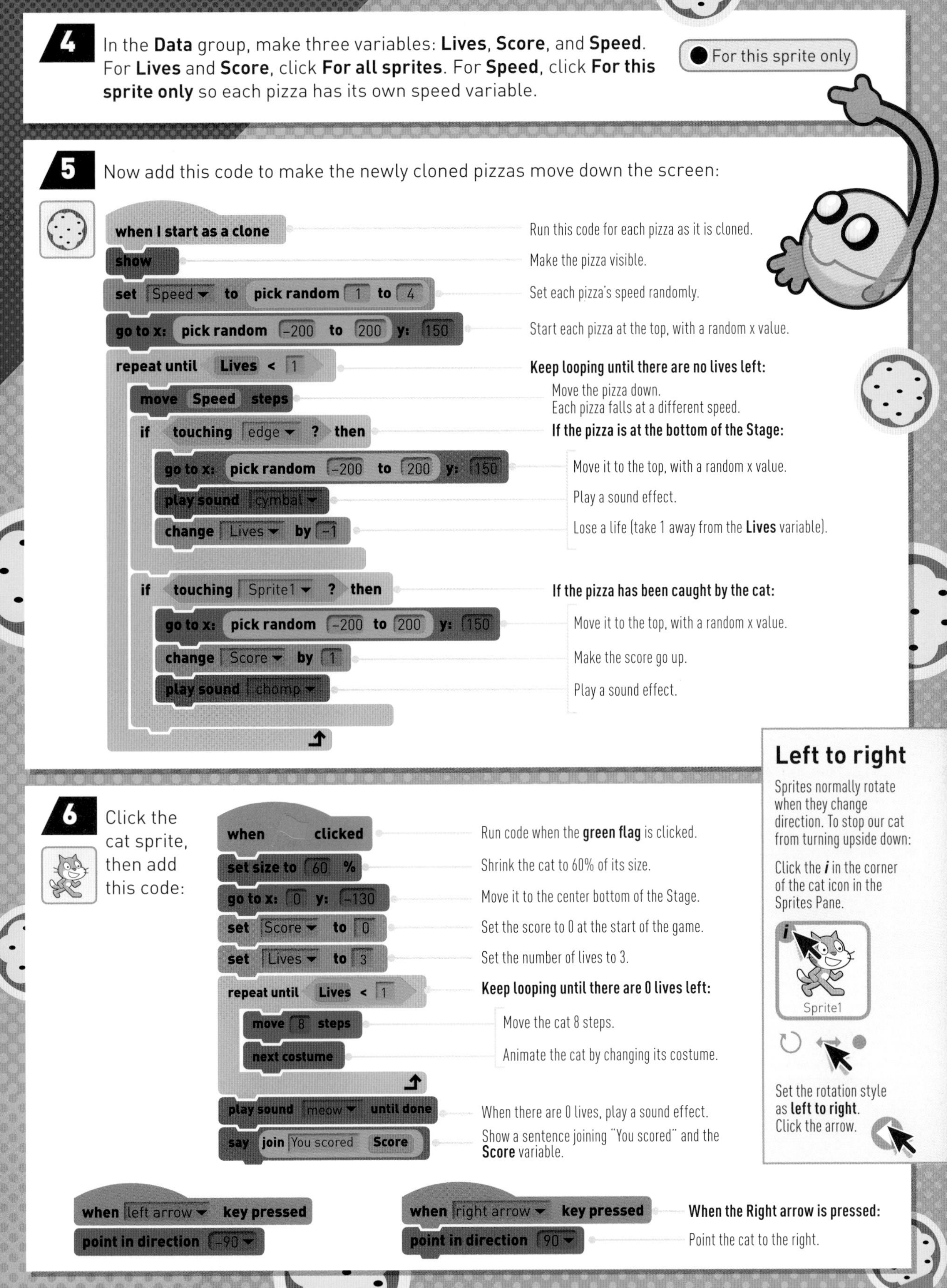

4 In the **Data** group, make three variables: **Lives**, **Score**, and **Speed**. For **Lives** and **Score**, click **For all sprites**. For **Speed**, click **For this sprite only** so each pizza has its own speed variable.

For this sprite only

5 Now add this code to make the newly cloned pizzas move down the screen:

```
when I start as a clone                          Run this code for each pizza as it is cloned.
show                                             Make the pizza visible.
set [Speed] to (pick random (1) to (4))          Set each pizza's speed randomly.
go to x: (pick random (-200) to (200)) y: (150)  Start each pizza at the top, with a random x value.
repeat until <(Lives) < (1)>                     Keep looping until there are no lives left:
    move (Speed) steps                           Move the pizza down. Each pizza falls at a different speed.
    if <touching [edge] ?> then                  If the pizza is at the bottom of the Stage:
        go to x: (pick random (-200) to (200)) y: (150)   Move it to the top, with a random x value.
        play sound [cymbal]                      Play a sound effect.
        change [Lives] by (-1)                   Lose a life (take 1 away from the Lives variable).
    if <touching [Sprite1] ?> then               If the pizza has been caught by the cat:
        go to x: (pick random (-200) to (200)) y: (150)   Move it to the top, with a random x value.
        change [Score] by (1)                    Make the score go up.
        play sound [chomp]                       Play a sound effect.
```

6 Click the cat sprite, then add this code:

```
when [green flag] clicked                  Run code when the green flag is clicked.
set size to (60) %                         Shrink the cat to 60% of its size.
go to x: (0) y: (-130)                     Move it to the center bottom of the Stage.
set [Score] to (0)                         Set the score to 0 at the start of the game.
set [Lives] to (3)                         Set the number of lives to 3.
repeat until <(Lives) < (1)>               Keep looping until there are 0 lives left:
    move (8) steps                         Move the cat 8 steps.
    next costume                           Animate the cat by changing its costume.
play sound [meow] until done               When there are 0 lives, play a sound effect.
say (join [You scored] (Score))            Show a sentence joining "You scored" and the Score variable.

when [left arrow] key pressed
point in direction (-90)

when [right arrow] key pressed             When the Right arrow is pressed:
point in direction (90)                    Point the cat to the right.
```

Left to right

Sprites normally rotate when they change direction. To stop our cat from turning upside down:

Click the ***i*** in the corner of the cat icon in the Sprites Pane.

Sprite1

Set the rotation style as **left to right**. Click the arrow.

ROCK BLASTER

In this space game, we will make two sets of clones. Our spaceship has to avoid the cloned rocks that are hurtling toward it. Luckily, we have a laser blaster to fire at the rocks. Each time we fire the laser, a clone of the laser is created. If a laser clone hits a rock, we get 100 points. But if a rock hits the spaceship, the game is over.

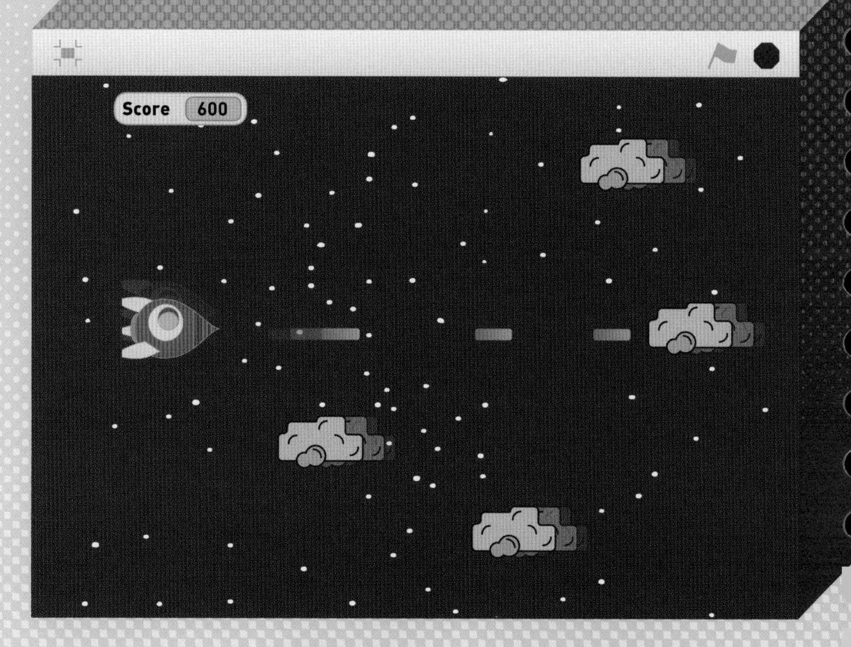

1 Click the **Stage** icon, then **Backdrops**.

Click **Choose backdrop from library**. Choose **Stars** then click **OK**.

2 Delete the cat sprite, then add a new sprite from the library called **Spaceship**. Click the *i* button on the new spaceship icon in the Sprites Pane.

Rotate the spaceship by dragging the direction handle around to **180 degrees**. Click the **triangle**.

3 Add two new sprites from the library. First, choose the one called **Rocks**.

Add a final sprite from the library, called **Button2**. This will be the laser.

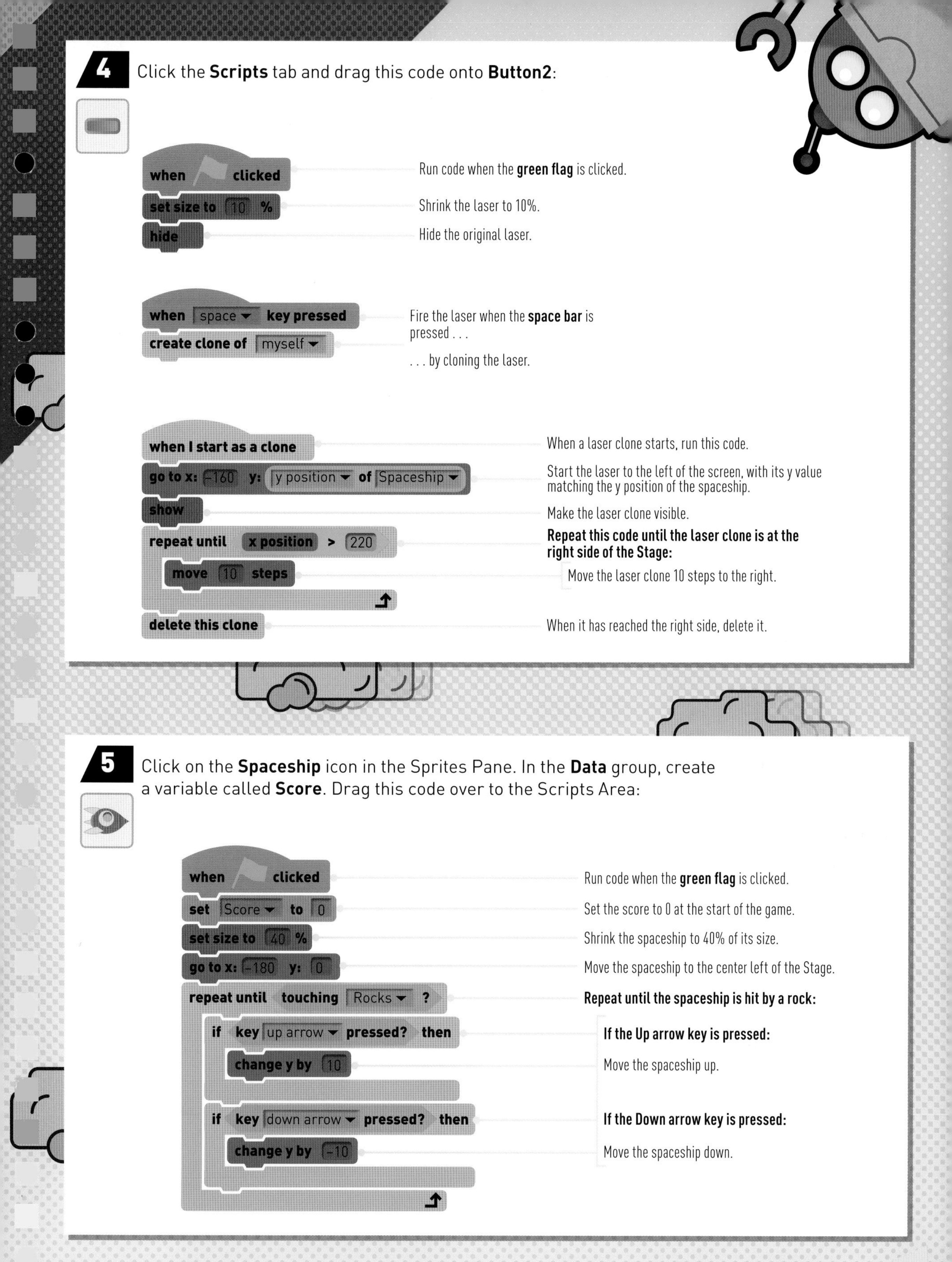

4 Click the **Scripts** tab and drag this code onto **Button2**:

```
when [green flag] clicked
set size to (10) %
hide
```

Run code when the **green flag** is clicked.

Shrink the laser to 10%.

Hide the original laser.

```
when [space ▾] key pressed
create clone of [myself ▾]
```

Fire the laser when the **space bar** is pressed . . .

. . . by cloning the laser.

```
when I start as a clone
go to x: (-160) y: ([y position ▾] of [Spaceship ▾])
show
repeat until <(x position) > (220)>
    move (10) steps
end
delete this clone
```

When a laser clone starts, run this code.

Start the laser to the left of the screen, with its y value matching the y position of the spaceship.

Make the laser clone visible.

Repeat this code until the laser clone is at the right side of the Stage:

Move the laser clone 10 steps to the right.

When it has reached the right side, delete it.

5 Click on the **Spaceship** icon in the Sprites Pane. In the **Data** group, create a variable called **Score**. Drag this code over to the Scripts Area:

```
when [green flag] clicked
set [Score ▾] to (0)
set size to (40) %
go to x: (-180) y: (0)
repeat until <touching [Rocks ▾] ?>
    if <key [up arrow ▾] pressed?> then
        change y by (10)
    end
    if <key [down arrow ▾] pressed?> then
        change y by (-10)
    end
end
```

Run code when the **green flag** is clicked.

Set the score to 0 at the start of the game.

Shrink the spaceship to 40% of its size.

Move the spaceship to the center left of the Stage.

Repeat until the spaceship is hit by a rock:

If the Up arrow key is pressed:

Move the spaceship up.

If the Down arrow key is pressed:

Move the spaceship down.

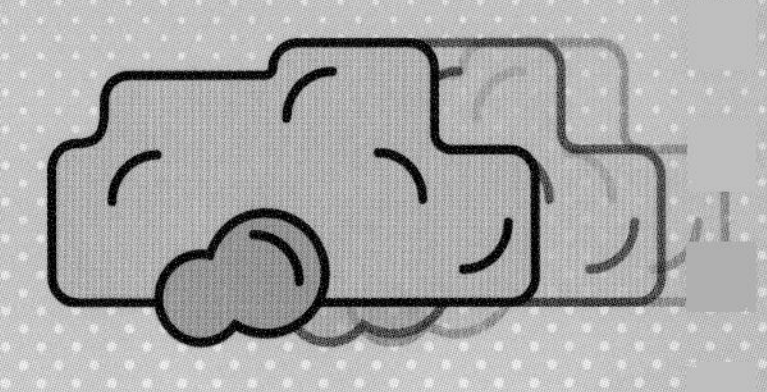

6

Click on the **Rocks** icon in the Sprites Pane. In the **Data** group, create another variable, called **Speed**—click **For this sprite only** so each rock has its own **Speed** variable. Create this code for the **Rocks** sprite:

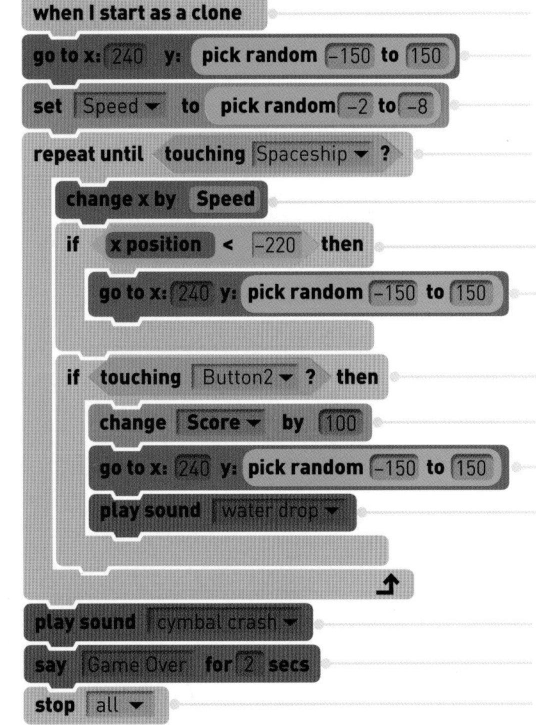

Run code when the **green flag** is clicked.

Show the rock.

Shrink the rock to 50% of its size.

Repeat this code four times to create four clones:

Clone a copy of the rock.

Hide the original rock.

When a rock clone starts, run the following code.

Position the rock clone on the right side of the Stage with a random y coordinate.

Set the speed randomly (to a negative number).

Repeat until the rock hits the spaceship:

Move the rock left according to the amount stored in its own **Speed** variable.

If it reaches the left side:

Move the rock back to the right side with a random y coordinate.

If the rock gets hit by a laser:

Increase the score by 100.

Move the rock back to the right side with a random y coordinate.

Play a sound effect.

When a rock hits the spaceship, play a sound effect.

Show "Game Over."

Stop all sprites moving.

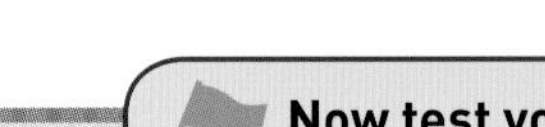

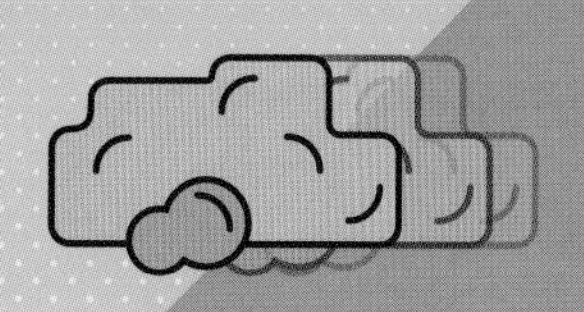

EXPERIMENT

- In step 4, find the code that moves the laser. Experiment with changing the number in the **Move 10 steps** block to much higher numbers. How does this change the laser? What happens if the number gets really big? Try 150! Does the laser always hit the rock? If so, why?

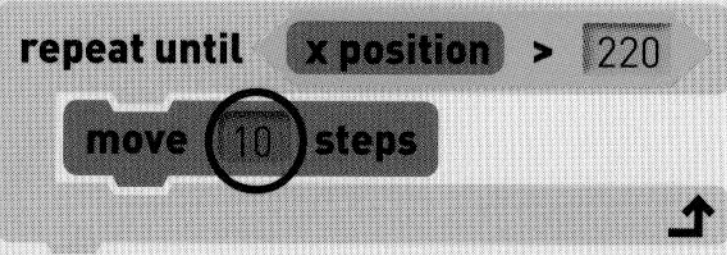

- Look at the code in step 5. Alter the amount y is changed by when you press the **Up** and **Down** arrow keys. Try changing it from 10 and –10 to 2 and –2, or 20 and –20. How does this change the game?

```
if key up arrow pressed? then
    change y by 10

if key down arrow pressed? then
    change y by -10
```

CHALLENGES

- Add more rocks to the game.
- Add an **If then** code block so a new rock is created when the score reaches a certain number.
- Make the rocks move faster as the score goes up. Hint: you could add a second **Change x by** block that moves by **Score** divided by a large negative number.
- Add a timer that shows how long the spaceship has survived before being hit by a rock.
- Draw a more exciting background for your game—let your imagination run wild.
- Create a new game of your own using what you have learned about clones.
- Change the sound effects used in the game. Can you make it sound more dramatic?

BALLOON BURSTER

In this quick-fire game, we will use cloning to make ten balloons. The balloons float across the screen from left to right while the player fires arrows at them, using the mouse for positioning. When the player hits a balloon, it bursts and the score goes up. After 30 seconds, the game is stopped by a timer. Take your aim quickly . . . ready . . . FIRE!

Score 5

1 Start a new file. **Right-click** the cat. (On older Macs, press **Ctrl**, then click.) Click **Delete**.

2 Click **Backdrops**. Using the **Fill** tool, make a sky background.

3 To start drawing your arrow, click the **Paint new sprite** button.

New sprite:

Choose the **Line** tool. Make the line thicker.

90%

Draw your arrow pointing to the right. Make it nearly as wide as the Drawing Area.

Fill the arrow head in.

4 Click the blue ***i*** on the arrow icon in the Sprites Pane.

Type in **Arrow** to name the sprite.

Then click the triangle.

Arrow

5 Click **Choose sprite from library**. Scroll down then click the **Balloon1** icon. Click **OK**.

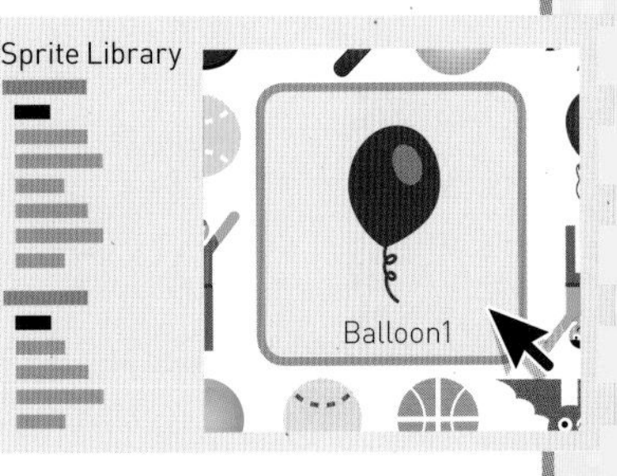

6

Click **Arrow** in the Sprites Pane, then click **Scripts**.

In the **Data** group, create a variable called **Score**. Then add this code to the arrow. Choose **Boing** from the **Sounds Library** under the **Sounds** tab.

```
when [green flag] clicked                   Run code when the green flag is clicked.
set [Score] to (0)                          Set the score to 0 at the start of the game.
reset timer                                 Rest the timer to 0 seconds at the start of the game.
set size to (15) %                          Shrink the arrow to 15% of its size.
go to x: (0) y: (-130)                      Start the arrow at the center bottom of the Stage.
repeat until <(timer) > (30)>               Repeat until 30 seconds is up:
    wait (0.2) secs                             Wait for a moment to get ready.
    repeat until <mouse down?>                  Repeat until the mouse is clicked:
        point towards [mouse-pointer]               Point the arrow toward the mouse.
    end
    play sound [boing]                          Play a sound effect when the mouse is clicked.
    repeat until <touching [edge] ?>            Repeat until the arrow reaches the edge:
        move (20) steps                             Move the arrow toward the mouse.
    end
    go to x: (0) y: (-130)                      The arrow has reached the edge of the Stage,
                                                so move it back to the start position.
end
say (join [You scored] (Score))             Show the score.
```

7

Now add this code to the balloon:

```
when [green flag] clicked                   Run code when the green flag is clicked.
hide                                        Hide the original balloon.
repeat (10)                                 Repeat this code ten times:
    create clone of [myself]                    Clone a copy of the balloon.
end
```

```
when I start as a clone                     When a balloon clone starts, run this code.
go to x: (pick random (-200) to (200)) y: (pick random (50) to (150))
                                            Position the balloon near the top of
                                            the Stage with a random x coordinate.
show                                        Make the balloon visible.
set size to (40) %                          Shrink the balloon to 40% of its size.
forever                                     Repeat this code forever:
    move (1) steps                              Move the balloon slowly to the right.
    if <touching [Arrow] ?> then                If it is hit by an arrow:
        change [Score] by (1)                       Increase the score by 1 point.
        play sound [pop]                            Play a sound effect.
        go to x: (pick random (-200) to (200)) y: (pick random (50) to (150))
                                                    Pick a new random position.
    end
    if <(x position) > (220)> then              If the balloon gets to the right of the Stage:
        go to x: (-200) y: (pick random (50) to (150))
                                                    Pick a random position on the left of the Stage.
        next costume                                Change the color of the balloon.
    end
end
```

Now test your code.

BRICK BOUNCER

Here the player has to bounce a ball against twenty cloned bricks. When the ball hits a brick, the brick disappears and the player gets five points. To bounce the ball, the player moves a bat at the bottom of the screen. The bat is moved as the mouse moves by setting its x coordinate to the x value of the mouse.

Score 10

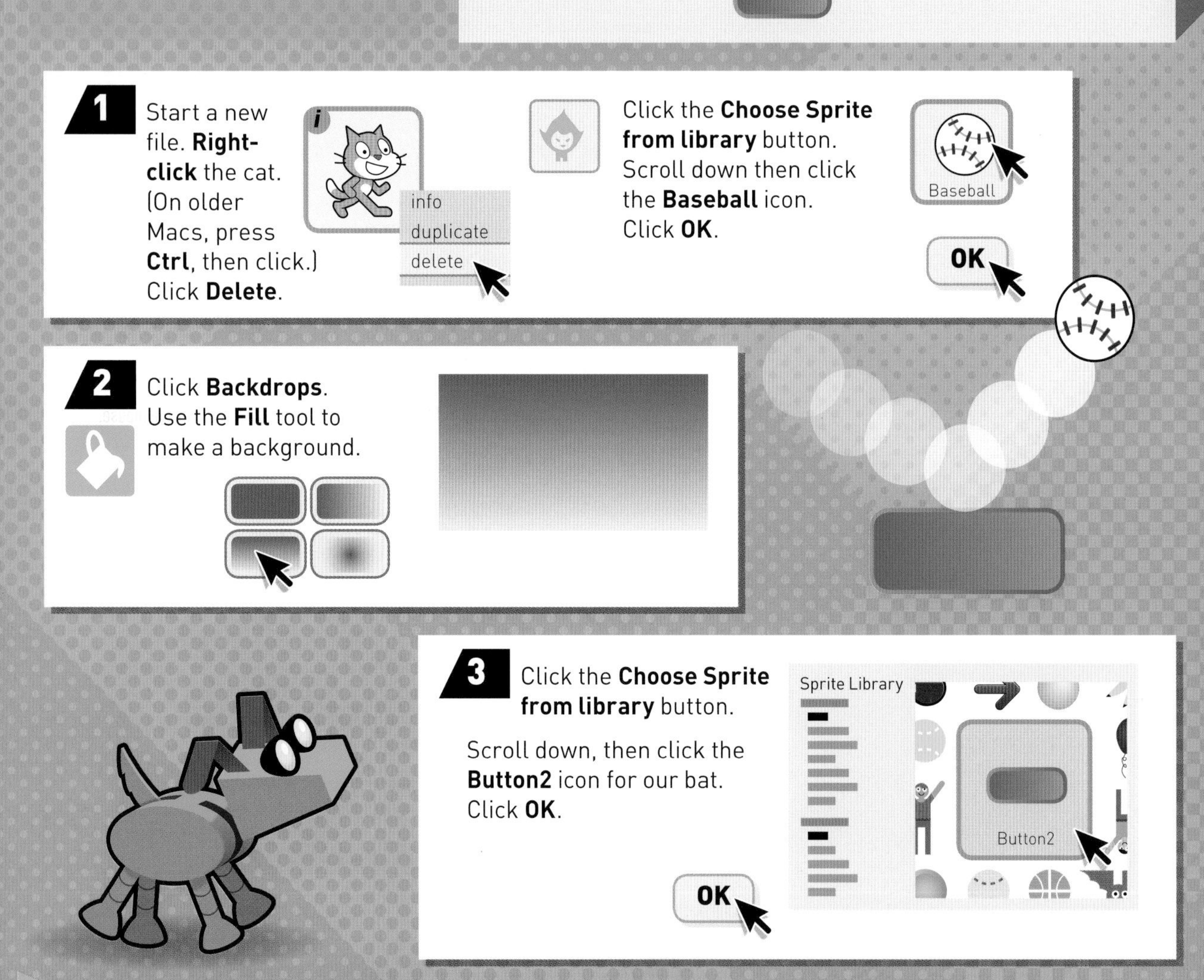

1 Start a new file. **Right-click** the cat. (On older Macs, press **Ctrl**, then click.) Click **Delete**.

Click the **Choose Sprite from library** button. Scroll down then click the **Baseball** icon. Click **OK**.

2 Click **Backdrops**. Use the **Fill** tool to make a background.

3 Click the **Choose Sprite from library** button.

Scroll down, then click the **Button2** icon for our bat. Click **OK**.

4

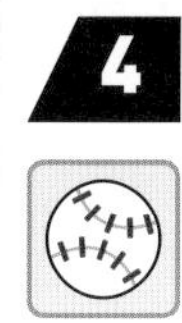

Click the **Baseball** icon, then **Scripts**. In the **Data** group, create a variable called **Score**. Choose sound effects from the **Sounds Library** under the **Sounds** tab. Add this code to the baseball:

```
when [flag] clicked
set Score to 0
set size to 50 %
point in direction 0
go to x: 0 y: -120
repeat until Score = 100
    if on edge, bounce
    move 8 steps
    if y position < -140 then
        say Game Over!
        play sound alien creak2 until done
        stop all
say Good job
```

- Run code when the **green flag** is clicked.
- Set the score to 0 at the start of the game.
- Shrink the baseball to 50% of its size.
- Point the baseball up (0 degrees).
- Start at the center bottom of the Stage.
- **Repeat this code until the score is 100:**
  - If the baseball hits the edge of the Stage, bounce off it.
  - Move the baseball forward.
  - **If the baseball reaches the bottom of the Stage:**
    - Show "Game Over!"
    - Play a sound effect.
  - Stop all the code running.
- When the score reaches 100, show "Good job."

5

Add this code to the bat:

```
when [flag] clicked
set y to -135
forever
    set x to mouse x
    if touching Baseball ? then
        broadcast Bounce
        play sound boing
```

- Run code when the **green flag** is clicked.
- Move the bat to the bottom of the Stage:
- **Repeat this code forever:**
  - Set the x value of the bat to be the same as the x value of the mouse.
  - **If the bat is touching the baseball:**
    - Broadcast "Bounce" so the ball knows what has happened.
    - Play a sound effect.

Use the drop-down menu to set this. Click "New message" then type "Bounce."

6

Now add this code to the baseball:

```
when I receive Bounce
turn C pick random 150 to 210 degrees
move 20 steps
```

- Run code when "Bounce" is broadcast.
- Turn the ball to go back in roughly the opposite direction.
- Move the ball 20 steps.

7 Now create a brick:

Click the **Paint new sprite** button.

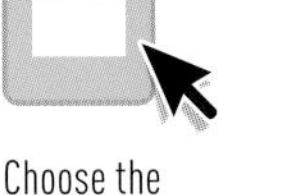

Choose the **Rectangle** tool.

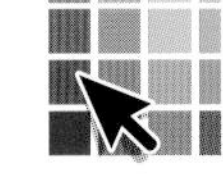

Pick dark red.

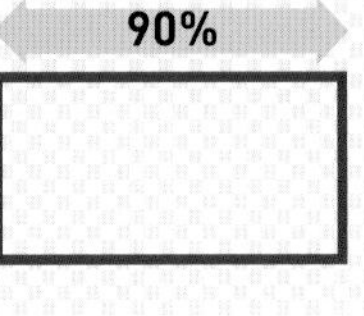

Draw a red rectangle that takes up most of the Drawing Area.

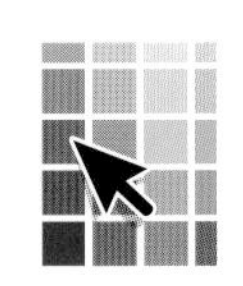

Choose red.

Fill the rectangle.

8 Add this code to the brick:

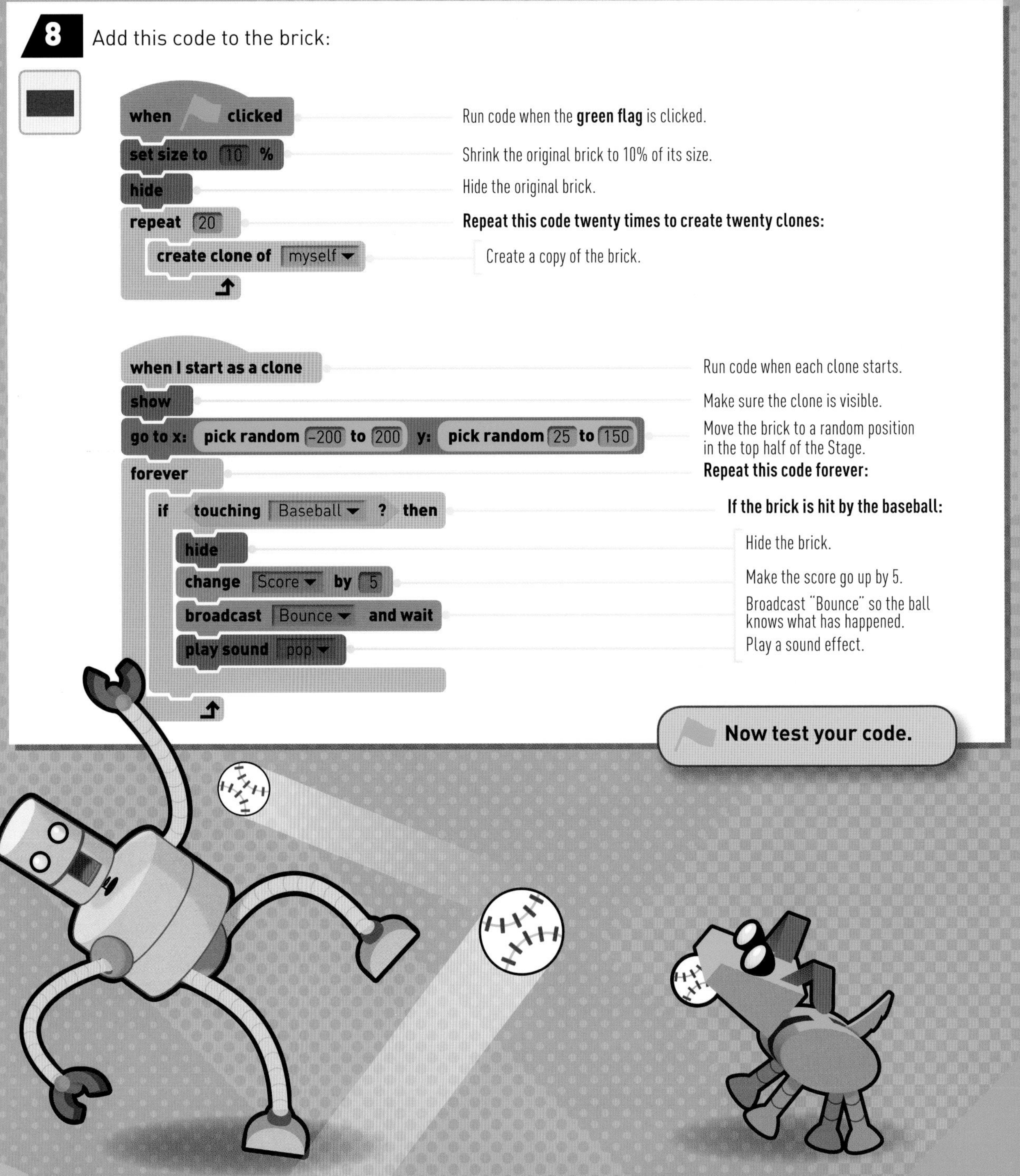

```
when [flag] clicked                      Run code when the green flag is clicked.
set size to (10) %                       Shrink the original brick to 10% of its size.
hide                                     Hide the original brick.
repeat (20)                              Repeat this code twenty times to create twenty clones:
    create clone of [myself ▼]               Create a copy of the brick.
```

```
when I start as a clone                  Run code when each clone starts.
show                                     Make sure the clone is visible.
go to x: (pick random (-200) to (200)) y: (pick random (25) to (150))
                                         Move the brick to a random position
                                         in the top half of the Stage.
forever                                  Repeat this code forever:
    if <touching [Baseball ▼] ?> then        If the brick is hit by the baseball:
        hide                                     Hide the brick.
        change [Score ▼] by (5)                  Make the score go up by 5.
        broadcast [Bounce ▼] and wait            Broadcast "Bounce" so the ball
                                                 knows what has happened.
        play sound [pop ▼]                       Play a sound effect.
```

Now test your code.

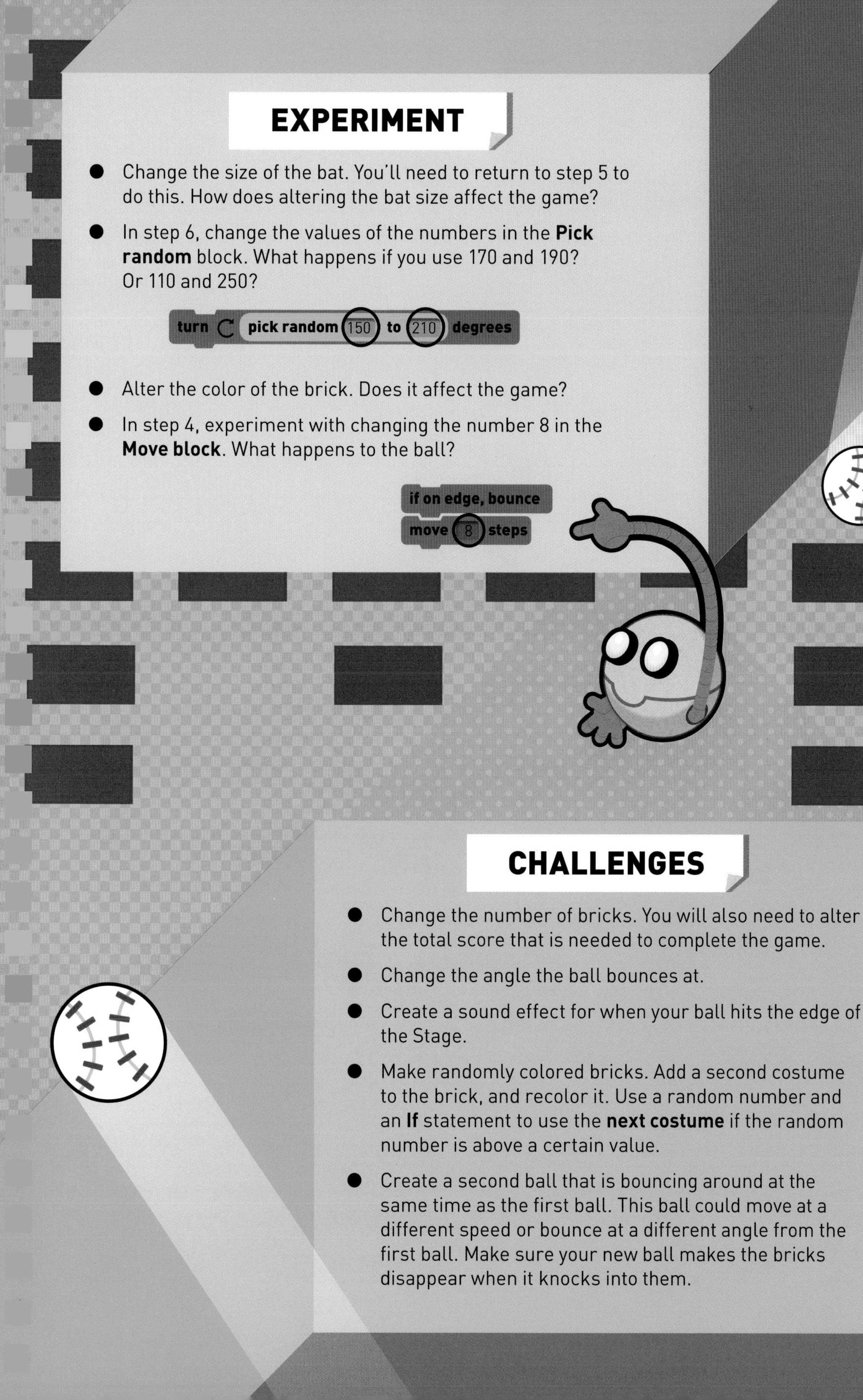

EXPERIMENT

- Change the size of the bat. You'll need to return to step 5 to do this. How does altering the bat size affect the game?
- In step 6, change the values of the numbers in the **Pick random** block. What happens if you use 170 and 190? Or 110 and 250?

turn pick random 150 to 210 degrees

- Alter the color of the brick. Does it affect the game?
- In step 4, experiment with changing the number 8 in the **Move block**. What happens to the ball?

if on edge, bounce
move 8 steps

CHALLENGES

- Change the number of bricks. You will also need to alter the total score that is needed to complete the game.
- Change the angle the ball bounces at.
- Create a sound effect for when your ball hits the edge of the Stage.
- Make randomly colored bricks. Add a second costume to the brick, and recolor it. Use a random number and an **If** statement to use the **next costume** if the random number is above a certain value.
- Create a second ball that is bouncing around at the same time as the first ball. This ball could move at a different speed or bounce at a different angle from the first ball. Make sure your new ball makes the bricks disappear when it knocks into them.

LEVEL 5 GAMES

In our expert-level games, we're going to make our sprites' movements even more complicated. They will fall and bounce in ways that mimic forces such as gravity. Code that mimics forces is called a "physics engine." When we're doing difficult things like this, our code could become really long. To stop that from happening, we will use "functions," so we don't have to keep repeating lines of code.

FUNCTIONS

A function is a set of commands created to do something special every time the function is run, or "called," such as make our penguin move to the starting point. What's useful about a function is that we don't have to keep recreating the code to tell the penguin to move to the start every time we need it to go there. We just create that code once.

Let's take a closer look at a function we'll use in *Penguin Jumper* (page 68). Before the penguin can jump, we need it to move to the land, set its speed to 0, and make sure it is pointing in the correct direction. We need to do that at the start of the game, and after every jump. Rather than entering the code twice, we create a function called **MovePenguinToStart**.

How to create a function:

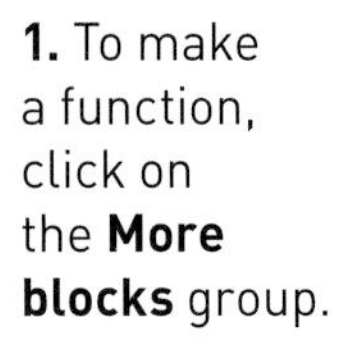

1. To make a function, click on the **More blocks** group.

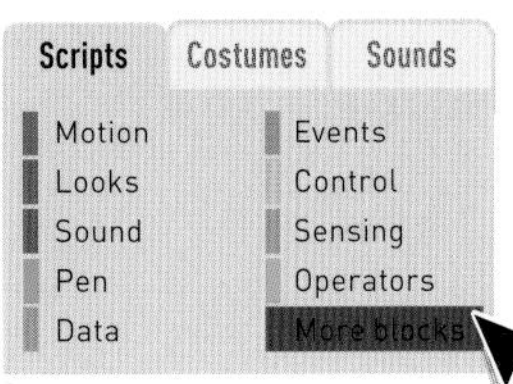

2. Click **Make a block**.

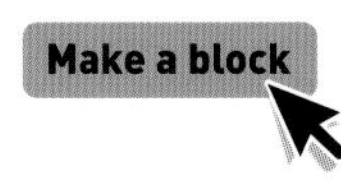

3. Type **MovePenguinToStart** as a name for your function.

Then click **OK**.

4. A new block that says **Define MovePenguinToStart** will appear in the Scripts Area.

5. Drag on a **Go to x y** block and any other code you want to run when the block is used.

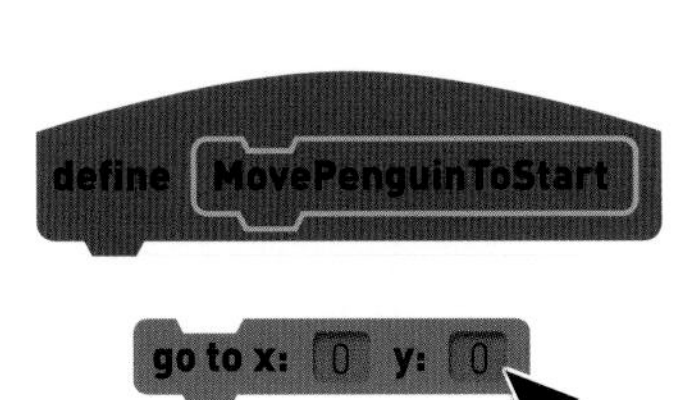

How to use a function:

1. To use a function you have created, click on the **More blocks** group.

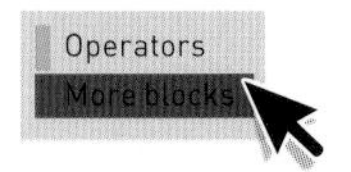

2. A block called **MovePenguinToStart** will be in the More Blocks group.

3. Drag the **MovePenguinToStart** block into your code where you need it.

JUMPING AND THROWING

In *Penguin Jumper*, we make a penguin jump onto an iceberg. In *Tower Smash* (page 72) we make a ball fly through the air.

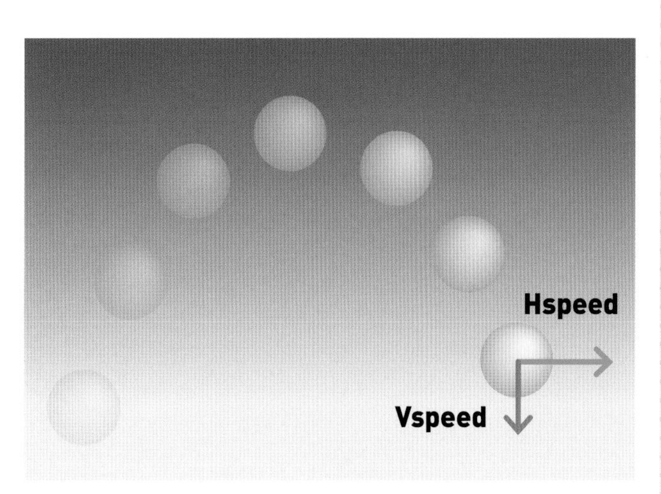

We can simulate jumping and throwing in a program by using two speed variables. One will be the vertical speed (**Vspeed**), which has to get more negative every loop to pull the ball or penguin toward the earth. This is the effect of gravity.

The other variable will be the horizontal speed (**Hspeed**). The horizontal speed needs to reduce slightly every loop because of friction and air resistance.

Take a look at the code we use to do all this:

```
change Vspeed by -0.2
set Hspeed to 0.99 * Hspeed
change x by Hspeed
change y by Vspeed
```

Make **Vspeed** decrease by 0.2.

Set Hspeed to 0.99 times **Hspeed** (* means multiply). This reduces it slightly.

Change the x position of the ball by the value of **Hspeed**.

Change the y position of the ball by the value of **Vspeed**.

BOUNCING

Once we are using horizontal and vertical speed variables, it is easy to make a ball bounce. If a ball is falling and hits the ground, we make it move up by changing **Vspeed** from a negative value (moving down) to a positive value (moving up).

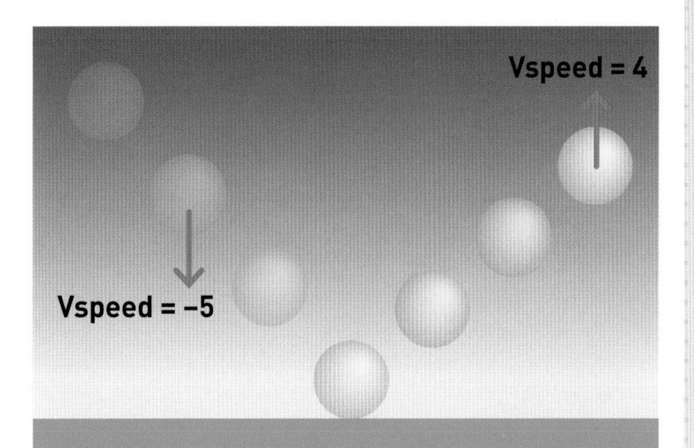

When things bounce, they usually slow down a little bit, too. In *Tower Smash* (page 72), we do all that with this piece of code:

```
if touching color [ ] ? then
    set Vspeed to -0.8 * Vspeed
```

If the ball hits the ground:

Make **Vspeed** = –0.8 times **Vspeed**. By multiplying by –0.8, we are changing a negative number (falling down) to a positive one (bouncing up), and reducing it a little bit.

Don't worry if you don't understand this code yet. Once you have coded the next two games, experiment with the numbers and see what happens. You'll soon figure it out!

PENGUIN JUMPER

The object of this game is for our penguin to jump onto an iceberg without landing in the water. The player chooses how fast and in what direction the penguin jumps by moving the purple arrow and then clicking the mouse. There is some math involved in moving the penguin, so we'll use functions to define how the penguin will start and how it will jump. This makes the code simpler to read and adapt.

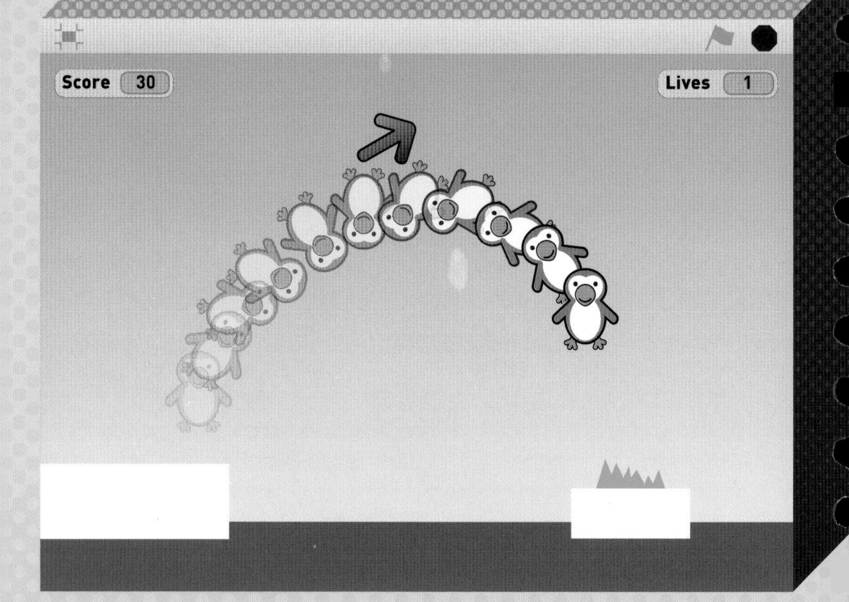

Before starting work on the computer, we will plan how the game will work.

Penguin Jumper: Plan

- Randomly position iceberg.
- Wait for player to tell penguin the jump direction and speed.
- Set starting speeds for penguin (horizontal and vertical).
- Main loop: until penguin hits iceberg or the sea/edge:
  - Move penguin.
  - Spin penguin.
  - Change speed.
- If penguin hits iceberg, give more points.
- If penguin misses, lose a life.
- If lives more than 0, do it again.

Jumping

We are going to use two variables to control the penguin's speed and direction: **Hspeed** (horizontal speed) and **Vspeed** (vertical speed).

If we want the penguin to be going up at a steep angle, we want the **Vspeed** value to be much larger than **Hspeed**. For example:

If we want the penguin to be going up more gently, we need the **Vspeed** value to be much smaller than **Hspeed**. For example:

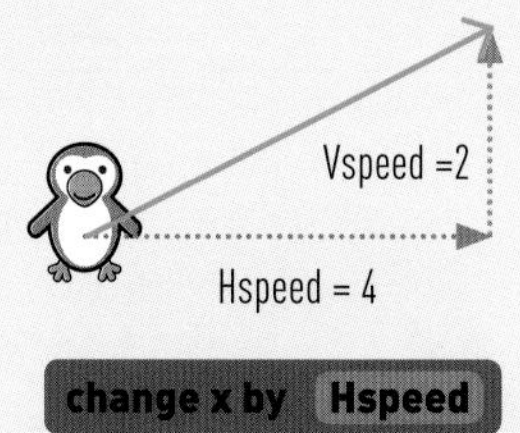

This code will move the penguin each loop:

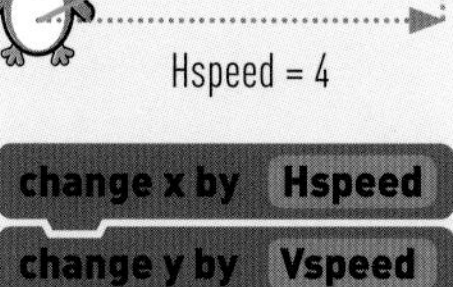

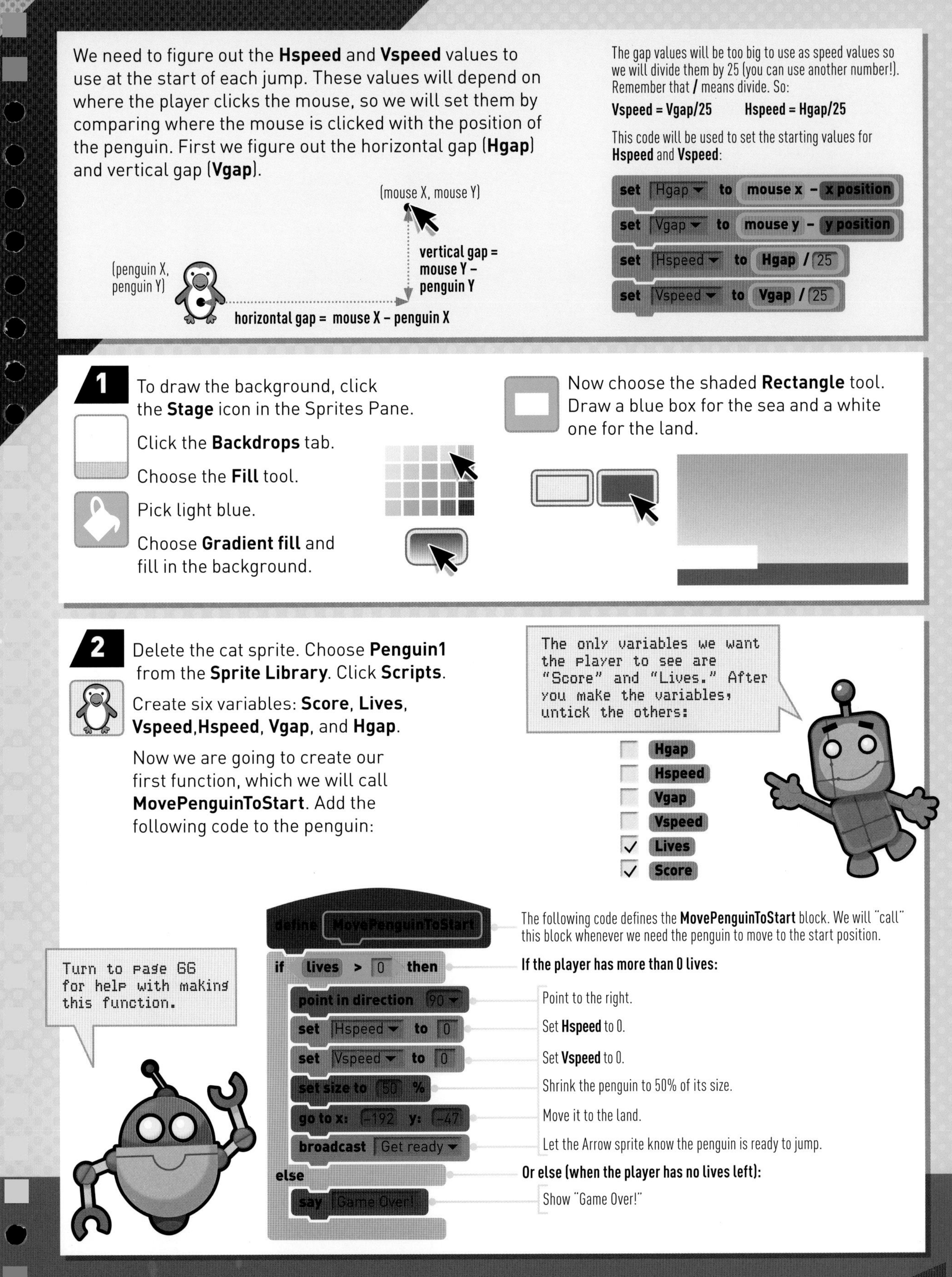

We need to figure out the **Hspeed** and **Vspeed** values to use at the start of each jump. These values will depend on where the player clicks the mouse, so we will set them by comparing where the mouse is clicked with the position of the penguin. First we figure out the horizontal gap (**Hgap**) and vertical gap (**Vgap**).

The gap values will be too big to use as speed values so we will divide them by 25 (you can use another number!). Remember that **/** means divide. So:

Vspeed = Vgap/25 **Hspeed = Hgap/25**

This code will be used to set the starting values for **Hspeed** and **Vspeed**:

```
set Hgap to mouse x - x position
set Vgap to mouse y - y position
set Hspeed to Hgap / 25
set Vspeed to Vgap / 25
```

1 To draw the background, click the **Stage** icon in the Sprites Pane.

Click the **Backdrops** tab.

Choose the **Fill** tool.

Pick light blue.

Choose **Gradient fill** and fill in the background.

Now choose the shaded **Rectangle** tool. Draw a blue box for the sea and a white one for the land.

2 Delete the cat sprite. Choose **Penguin1** from the **Sprite Library**. Click **Scripts**.

Create six variables: **Score**, **Lives**, **Vspeed**,**Hspeed**, **Vgap**, and **Hgap**.

Now we are going to create our first function, which we will call **MovePenguinToStart**. Add the following code to the penguin:

The only variables we want the player to see are "Score" and "Lives." After you make the variables, untick the others:

- [ ] Hgap
- [ ] Hspeed
- [ ] Vgap
- [ ] Vspeed
- [x] Lives
- [x] Score

Turn to page 66 for help with making this function.

```
define MovePenguinToStart
if lives > 0 then
    point in direction 90
    set Hspeed to 0
    set Vspeed to 0
    set size to 50 %
    go to x: -192 y: -47
    broadcast Get ready
else
    say Game Over!
```

The following code defines the **MovePenguinToStart** block. We will "call" this block whenever we need the penguin to move to the start position.

If the player has more than 0 lives:

Point to the right.

Set **Hspeed** to 0.

Set **Vspeed** to 0.

Shrink the penguin to 50% of its size.

Move it to the land.

Let the Arrow sprite know the penguin is ready to jump.

Or else (when the player has no lives left):

Show "Game Over!"

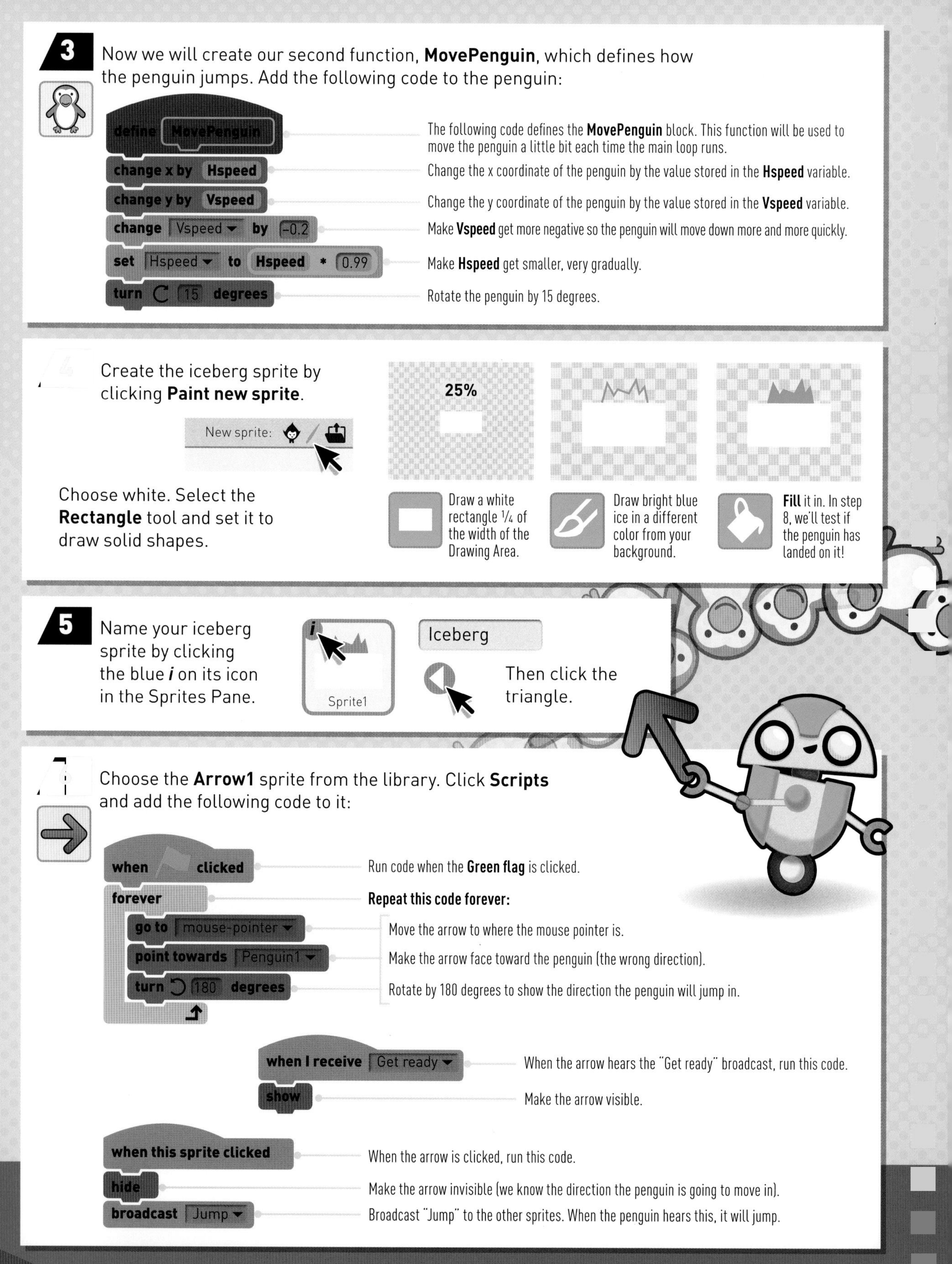

3

Now we will create our second function, **MovePenguin**, which defines how the penguin jumps. Add the following code to the penguin:

```
define MovePenguin
change x by Hspeed
change y by Vspeed
change Vspeed by -0.2
set Hspeed to Hspeed * 0.99
turn ↻ 15 degrees
```

- **define MovePenguin**: The following code defines the **MovePenguin** block. This function will be used to move the penguin a little bit each time the main loop runs.
- **change x by Hspeed**: Change the x coordinate of the penguin by the value stored in the **Hspeed** variable.
- **change y by Vspeed**: Change the y coordinate of the penguin by the value stored in the **Vspeed** variable.
- **change Vspeed by -0.2**: Make **Vspeed** get more negative so the penguin will move down more and more quickly.
- **set Hspeed to Hspeed * 0.99**: Make **Hspeed** get smaller, very gradually.
- **turn ↻ 15 degrees**: Rotate the penguin by 15 degrees.

4

Create the iceberg sprite by clicking **Paint new sprite**.

Choose white. Select the **Rectangle** tool and set it to draw solid shapes.

Draw a white rectangle ¼ of the width of the Drawing Area.

Draw bright blue ice in a different color from your background.

Fill it in. In step 8, we'll test if the penguin has landed on it!

5

Name your iceberg sprite by clicking the blue ***i*** on its icon in the Sprites Pane.

Then click the triangle.

6

Choose the **Arrow1** sprite from the library. Click **Scripts** and add the following code to it:

```
when [green flag] clicked
forever
    go to mouse-pointer
    point towards Penguin1
    turn ↺ 180 degrees
```

- **when [green flag] clicked**: Run code when the **Green flag** is clicked.
- **forever**: **Repeat this code forever:**
  - **go to mouse-pointer**: Move the arrow to where the mouse pointer is.
  - **point towards Penguin1**: Make the arrow face toward the penguin (the wrong direction).
  - **turn ↺ 180 degrees**: Rotate by 180 degrees to show the direction the penguin will jump in.

```
when I receive Get ready
show
```

- **when I receive Get ready**: When the arrow hears the "Get ready" broadcast, run this code.
- **show**: Make the arrow visible.

```
when this sprite clicked
hide
broadcast Jump
```

- **when this sprite clicked**: When the arrow is clicked, run this code.
- **hide**: Make the arrow invisible (we know the direction the penguin is going to move in).
- **broadcast Jump**: Broadcast "Jump" to the other sprites. When the penguin hears this, it will jump.

7 Add this code to the **Iceberg** sprite:

```
when I receive [Get ready ▼]
set x to (pick random (20) to (200))
set y to (-110)
```

When the iceberg hears the "Get ready" broadcast it will run this code.

Move the iceberg to a random left-to-right position.

Position it on the sea.

8 Click on the **Penguin1** icon in the Sprites Pane and add this code to it:

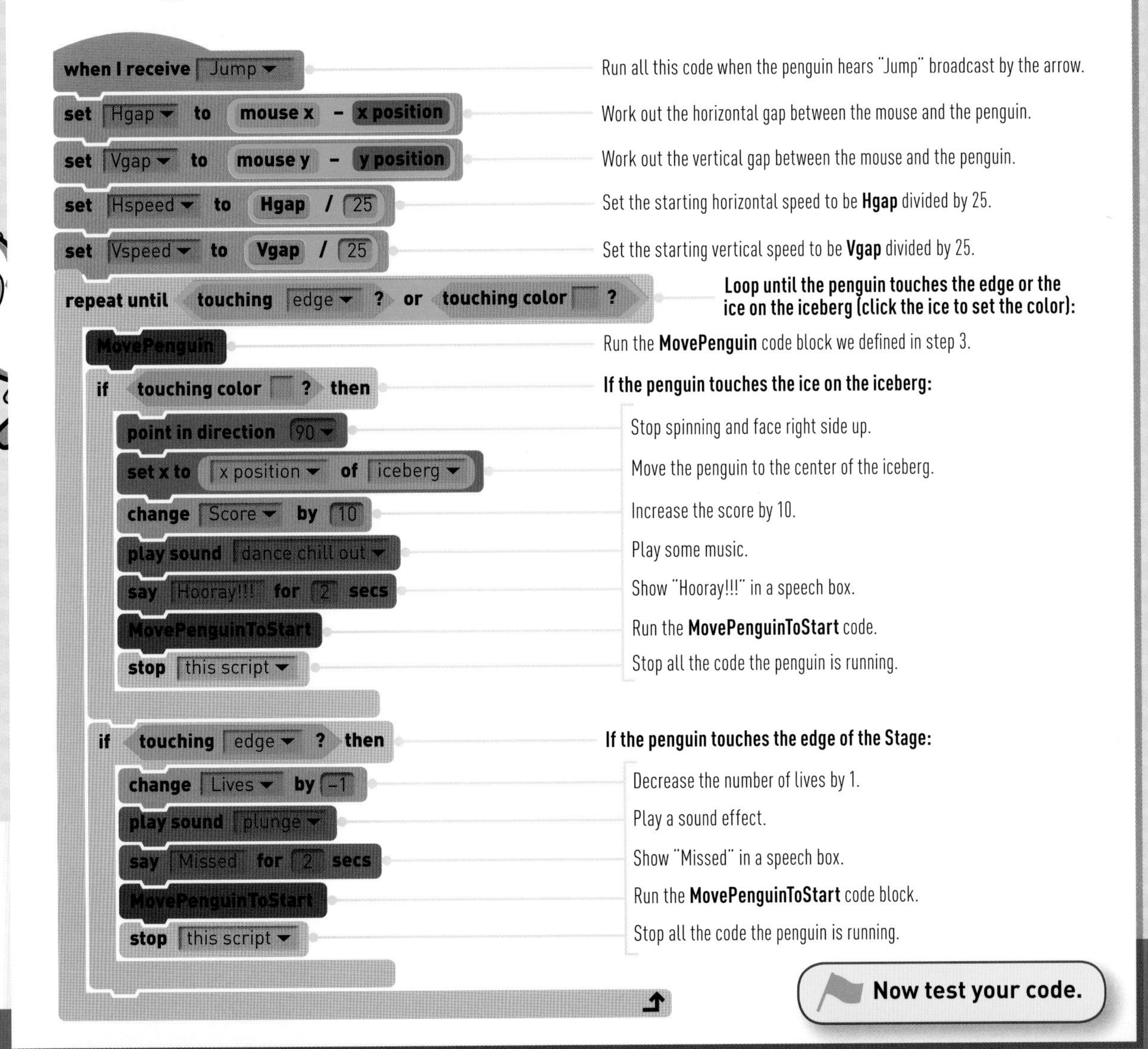

when clicked
set Score to 0
set Lives to 3
MovePenguinToStart
Run code when the green flag is clicked.
Set the score to 0 at the start of the game.
Set the number of lives to 3 at the start of the game.
Call the MovePenguinToStart code block. This will run all the code we created in step 2.
when I receive Jump
set Hgap to mouse x - x position
set Vgap to mouse y - y position
set Hspeed to Hgap / 25
set Vspeed to Vgap / 25
repeat until touching edge ? or touching color ?
MovePenguin
if touching color ? then
point in direction 90
set x to x position of iceberg
change Score by 10
play sound dance chill out
say Hooray!!! for 2 secs
MovePenguinToStart
stop this script
if touching edge ? then
change Lives by -1
play sound plunge
say Missed for 2 secs
MovePenguinToStart
stop this script
Run all this code when the penguin hears "Jump" broadcast by the arrow.
Work out the horizontal gap between the mouse and the penguin.
Work out the vertical gap between the mouse and the penguin.
Set the starting horizontal speed to be Hgap divided by 25.
Set the starting vertical speed to be Vgap divided by 25.
Loop until the penguin touches the edge or the ice on the iceberg (click the ice to set the color):
Run the MovePenguin code block we defined in step 3.
If the penguin touches the ice on the iceberg:
Stop spinning and face right side up.
Move the penguin to the center of the iceberg.
Increase the score by 10.
Play some music.
Show "Hooray!!!" in a speech box.
Run the MovePenguinToStart code.
Stop all the code the penguin is running.
If the penguin touches the edge of the Stage:
Decrease the number of lives by 1.
Play a sound effect.
Show "Missed" in a speech box.
Run the MovePenguinToStart code block.
Stop all the code the penguin is running.

Now test your code.

TOWER SMASH

In our final game, the player has to knock down a tower of blocks. This is done by firing a ball with a catapult. The code to make the ball move is similar to in *Penguin Jumper* (page 68), using horizontal and vertical speeds. The blocks are created by cloning. They have a very simple "physics engine," which makes them fall down the screen until they hit another block or the ground.

First of all, let's plan out how the game will work.
We need a variable to count how many blocks there are (Blockcount) and one to count the number of launches the player takes (Launches).

Tower Smash: Plan

- Create tower.
- Draw catapult with a thick orange line from the ball to the mouse. Clear, then draw line again when the mouse moves.
- Wait for player to fire ball with catapult.
- Set starting speeds for ball (horizontal and vertical).
- Main loop: until ball stops moving (or is very slow):
  - Move ball.
  - Change speed.
- If ball hits block, make block hide. Get points.
- Keep going until no blocks are left.

We need eight variables. The only variable we want the player to see is **Score**. After you make the variables, untick the others:

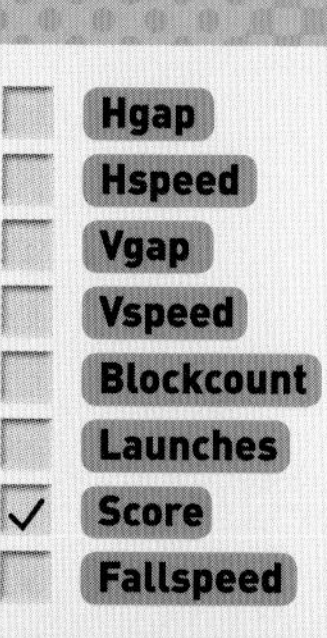

Making the ball move and bounce

We can make the ball move using similar code to the penguin in the previous game. For an explanation of how this works, see pages 68–69.

Unlike the penguin, our ball bounces! Turn to page 67 to find out how **Vspeed** and **Hspeed** can create bouncing.

If the ball touches the edge of the Stage, we need to stop it and get it ready for the next launch. We will also use a timer to return the ball to the start after five seconds, so it doesn't roll around for too long.

Falling blocks

We will store how fast each block falls in a variable called **Fallspeed**. When making this variable, set it to **For this sprite only** so that each block has its own speed.

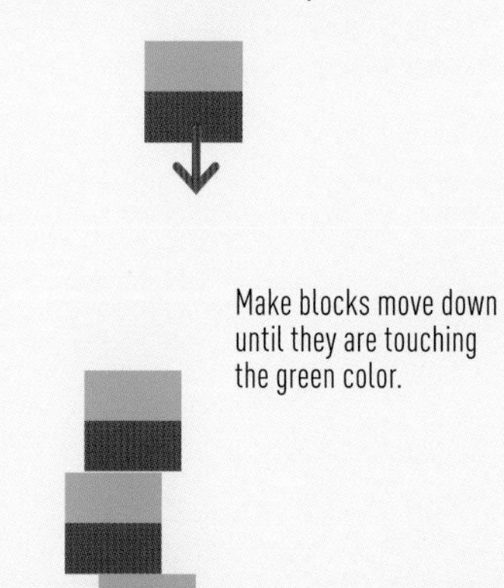

Make blocks move down until they are touching the green color.

1 To draw the background, click the **Stage** icon in the Sprites Pane.

Click the **Backdrops** tab.

Choose the **Fill** tool.

Pick light blue.

Choose **Gradient fill** and fill in the background.

Now choose the solid **Rectangle** tool.

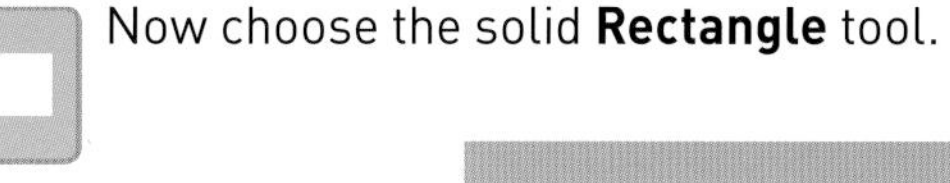

Draw a wide, thin, green block for grass. Use the second darkest green color. Below it, draw a brown block for earth.

2 Delete the cat sprite. Choose the **Ball** sprite from the library. Click on **Scripts**.

Now we will define our first function. We will call it **MoveBallToStart**. For help with making functions, turn to page 66.

```
define MoveBallToStart
go to x (-210) y: (-110)
set size to (50) %
set [Hspeed ▾] to (0)
set [Vspeed ▾] to (0)
broadcast [GetReady ▾]
```

The following code defines our **MoveBallToStart** block. We will run (or "call") this block whenever we need the ball to move to the start position.

Move the ball to the bottom left of the Stage.

Shrink it to 50% of its size.

Set **Hspeed** (horizontal speed) to 0.

Set **Vspeed** (vertical speed) to 0.

Broadcast "GetReady" to all the other sprites.

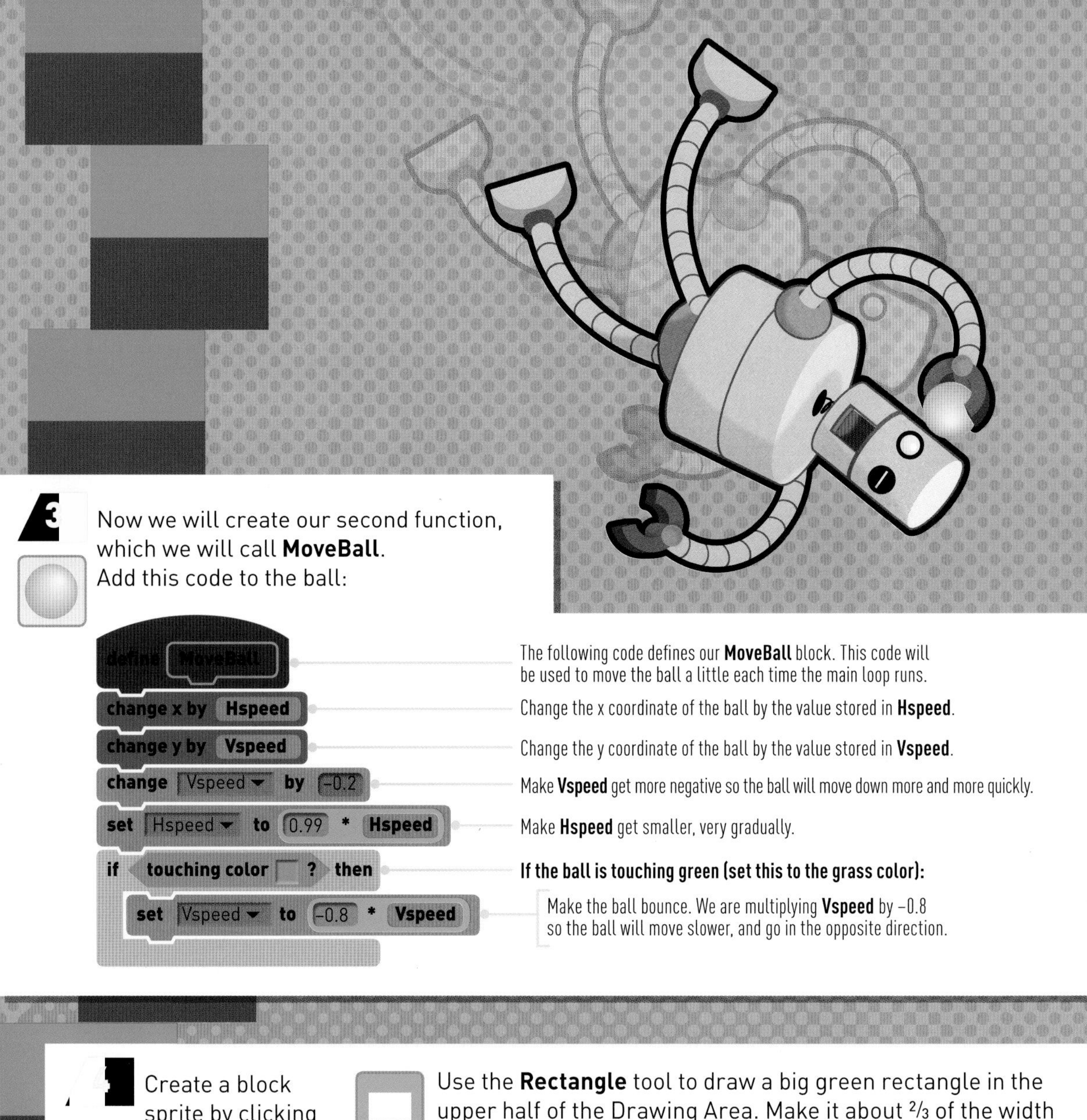

3 Now we will create our second function, which we will call **MoveBall**.
Add this code to the ball:

```
define MoveBall
change x by Hspeed
change y by Vspeed
change [Vspeed ▼] by (-0.2)
set [Hspeed ▼] to ((0.99) * (Hspeed))
if <touching color [ ] ?> then
    set [Vspeed ▼] to ((-0.8) * (Vspeed))
end
```

The following code defines our **MoveBall** block. This code will be used to move the ball a little each time the main loop runs.

Change the x coordinate of the ball by the value stored in **Hspeed**.

Change the y coordinate of the ball by the value stored in **Vspeed**.

Make **Vspeed** get more negative so the ball will move down more and more quickly.

Make **Hspeed** get smaller, very gradually.

If the ball is touching green (set this to the grass color):

Make the ball bounce. We are multiplying **Vspeed** by −0.8 so the ball will move slower, and go in the opposite direction.

4 Create a block sprite by clicking the **Paint new sprite** button.

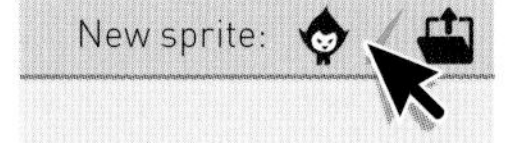

Use the **Rectangle** tool to draw a big green rectangle in the upper half of the Drawing Area. Make it about ⅔ of the width of the Drawing Area. Use the same color as for your grass.

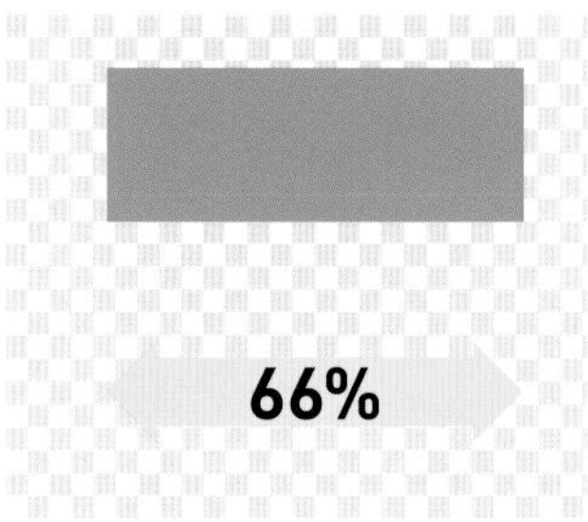

Draw a darker green rectangle underneath the first one.

5

We will now create a third function, called **CreatePile**.
Add this code to the block sprite:

```
define CreatePile
set Blockcount to 0
repeat 10
    create clone of myself
    change Blockcount by 1
hide
```

- The following code defines the **CreatePile** block. This code will be used to make the pile of blocks.
- Set Blockcount to 0. (Blockcount will count blocks as they are made and help position them.)
- **Repeat this ten times:**
  - Make a clone of the original block.
  - Increase the value of Blockcount by 1.
- Hide the original block.

Then add these two sets of code:

```
when [green flag] clicked
set size to 10 %
show
CreatePile
```

- Run code when the **green flag** is clicked.
- Shrink the original block to 10% of its size.
- Make the original block visible.
- Call the **CreatePile** function to make all the blocks.

Make sure the "Fallspeed" variable is set to "For this sprite only."

```
when I start as a clone
set Fallspeed to 0
go to x: pick random 180 to 200 y: -154 + Blockcount * 35
repeat until Blockcount = 0
    if touching Ball ? then
        hide
        change Score by Launches
        change Blockcount by -1
        play sound pop
        set Hspeed to -0.8 * Hspeed
    if not touching color [ ] ? then
        change Fallspeed by -0.1
        change y by Fallspeed
broadcast Completed Game
```

- Run this code when each block clone is created.
- Set Fallspeed to 0.
- Give the block a random x position, but make the y values go up with Blockcount.
- **Loop until no blocks are left:**
  - **If the ball has hit the block:**
    - Hide the block.
    - Increase the score, with a bonus for early hits.
    - Decrease the number of blocks left.
    - Play a sound effect.
    - Bounce the ball.
  - **If the ball has not hit anything green (set the color by clicking on the grass):**
    - Slightly increase the value of **Fallspeed**.
    - Move the ball down by the value of **Fallspeed**. As **Fallspeed** gets more negative, the ball will fall naturally, mimicking gravity.
- If there are no balls left, broadcast "Completed Game" so the other sprites know.

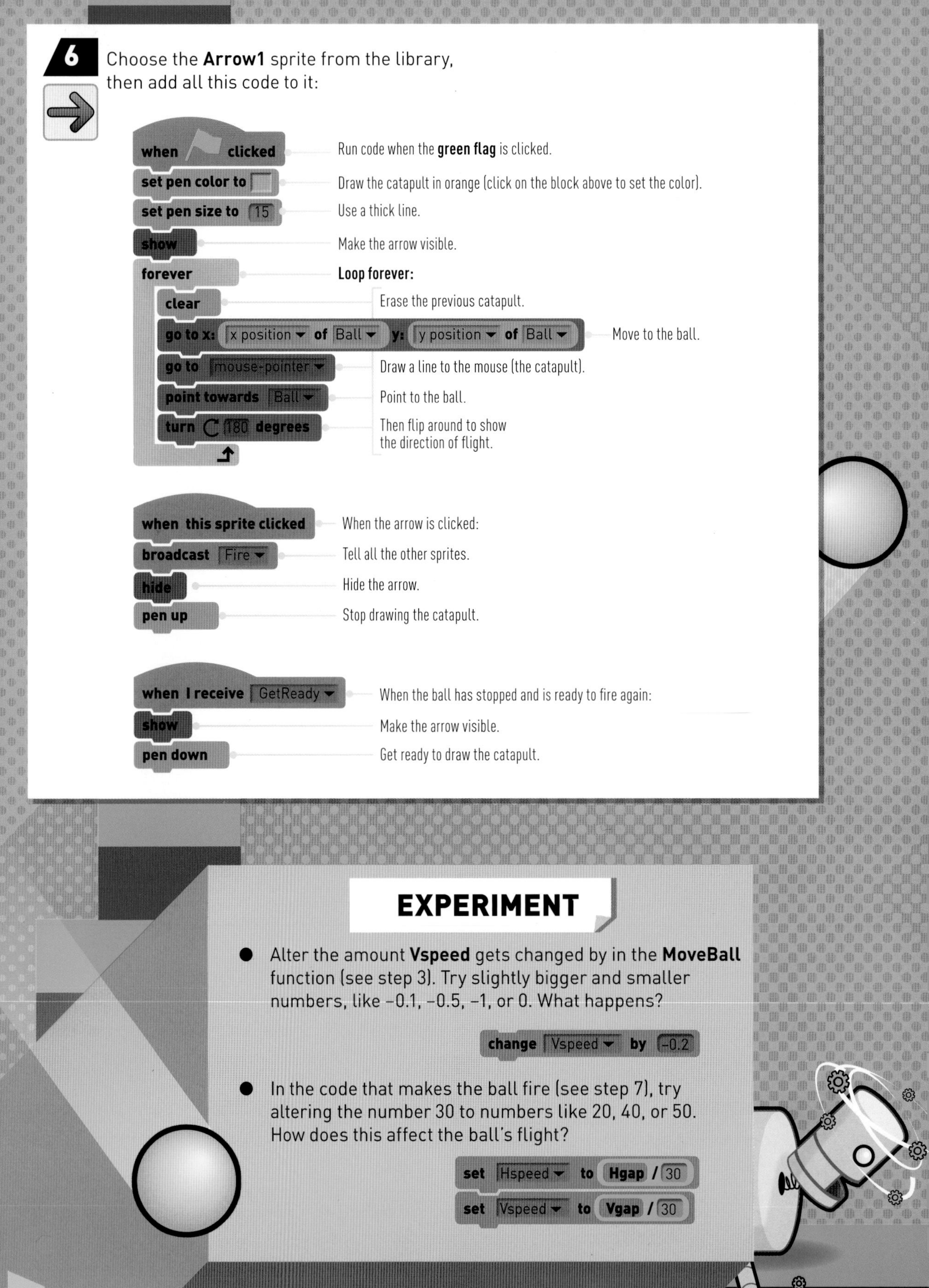

6 Choose the **Arrow1** sprite from the library, then add all this code to it:

```
when green flag clicked          Run code when the green flag is clicked.
set pen color to [ ]             Draw the catapult in orange (click on the block above to set the color).
set pen size to (15)             Use a thick line.
show                             Make the arrow visible.
forever                          Loop forever:
    clear                        Erase the previous catapult.
    go to x: (x position of Ball) y: (y position of Ball)    Move to the ball.
    go to [mouse-pointer]        Draw a line to the mouse (the catapult).
    point towards [Ball]         Point to the ball.
    turn ↻ (180) degrees         Then flip around to show the direction of flight.
```

```
when this sprite clicked         When the arrow is clicked:
broadcast [Fire]                 Tell all the other sprites.
hide                             Hide the arrow.
pen up                           Stop drawing the catapult.
```

```
when I receive [GetReady]        When the ball has stopped and is ready to fire again:
show                             Make the arrow visible.
pen down                         Get ready to draw the catapult.
```

EXPERIMENT

- Alter the amount **Vspeed** gets changed by in the **MoveBall** function (see step 3). Try slightly bigger and smaller numbers, like −0.1, −0.5, −1, or 0. What happens?

```
change [Vspeed] by (-0.2)
```

- In the code that makes the ball fire (see step 7), try altering the number 30 to numbers like 20, 40, or 50. How does this affect the ball's flight?

```
set [Hspeed] to (Hgap / 30)
set [Vspeed] to (Vgap / 30)
```

7 Finally, add all this code to the ball:

```
when [flag] clicked
set [Score] to [0]
set [Launches] to [20]
MoveBallToStart
```

- Run code when the **green flag** is clicked.
- Set the score to 0 at the start of the game.
- Set the number of launches to 20.
- Call (run) the **MoveBallToStart** function that we built in step 2.

```
when I receive [Fire]
reset timer
change [Launches] by (-1)
set [Hgap] to ((mouse x) - (x position))
set [Vgap] to ((mouse y) - (y position))
set [Hspeed] to ((Hgap) / (30))
set [Vspeed] to ((Vgap) / (30))
repeat until <<(timer) > [5]> or <touching [edge] ?>>
    MoveBall
end
MoveBallToStart
```

- The mouse has been clicked, so run this code:
- Start timing how long the ball moves for.
- Reduce the launch count.
- Figure out the horizontal gap between the mouse and ball.
- Figure out the vertical gap between the mouse and ball.
- Set the starting horizontal speed to be **Hgap** divided by 30.
- Set the starting vertical speed to be **Vgap** divided by 30.
- **Loop until the ball hits the edge or 5 seconds have passed:**
- Call the **MoveBall** function we made in step 3.
- The ball has hit the edge or moved for more than 5 seconds, so call the **MoveBallToStart** function.

```
when I receive [Completed Game]
say (join [You scored:] (Score))
```

- The game is complete, so run this code:
- Show "You scored:" and the score.

Now test your code!

CHALLENGES

- The **Launches** variable is used to give a bonus for knocking the blocks down quickly. Add code to stop the game when there are no launches left.
- Add instructions that will appear at the start of the game.
- Add sound effects.
- Add more blocks to the game. To make them fit on the screen, you may need to change the random values for the x position of the blocks.
- Make your own version of a jumping-animal or tower-smash game using functions to run parts of the code.

MAKING YOUR OWN GAMES

Just like writing a story, creating a game takes planning. You can plan in your head, on paper, or by coding. However you do it, think about these ideas . . . .

SETTING

Where is your game set? Is the game background just a picture, or will it need to stop the player from moving?

Look at page 15, step 5, or page 24 for how to draw a background. See page 54, step 1 for how to choose a background from the library.

You could use a **Repeat until** loop to move a sprite until it touches a particular color. *Drive Me Crazy* on pages 18–21 does that. *Snake* on pages 44–45 uses a more powerful method.

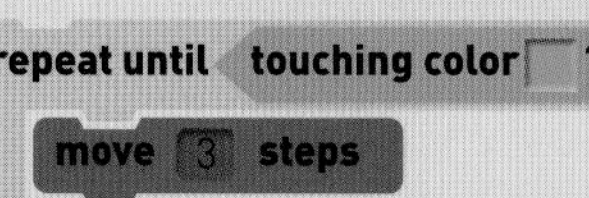

repeat until touching color ?
move 3 steps

PLAYER

Who or what is the player? An animal, human, robot, or car?

AIM OF THE GAME

What is the aim of the game? To collect lots of objects? To avoid bad guys for as long as possible? To get to a particular place? To do something as fast as possible? To score as many points as you can in a certain amount of time?

Turn to *Catch the Donut* on pages 30–31 for an example of a collecting game. In *Cat and Mouse* on pages 52–53, your sprite has to avoid bad guys. In *Cross the Road* on pages 24–25, you need to reach a particular place. Page 23, step 5 shows how to put a time limit on a game.

MOVEMENT

How will the player move? By following the mouse? By pressing keys to move up, down, left, and right? By steering left and right, like a car?

To follow the mouse:

```
forever
    point towards [mouse-pointer ▾]
    move (4) steps
```

Add this code to your sprite to make it follow the mouse. The number in the **Move steps** block controls how fast the sprite moves.

To press a key:

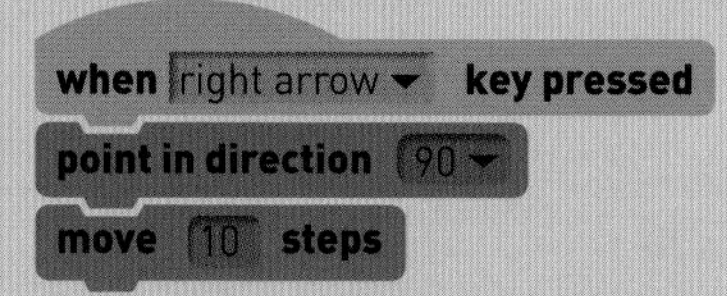

```
when [right arrow ▾] key pressed
point in direction (90 ▾)
move (10) steps
```

Choose your key using the drop-down menu on the **When key pressed** block. Pick the direction to move in with the drop-down menu on the **Point in direction** block.

To steer and rotate:

```
if <key [left arrow ▾] pressed?> then
    turn ↺ (5) degrees
```

Add this code to your sprite to make it rotate. Choose the key to press, and how far (or fast) to turn. You'll also need to add code somewhere else to make the sprite move forward.

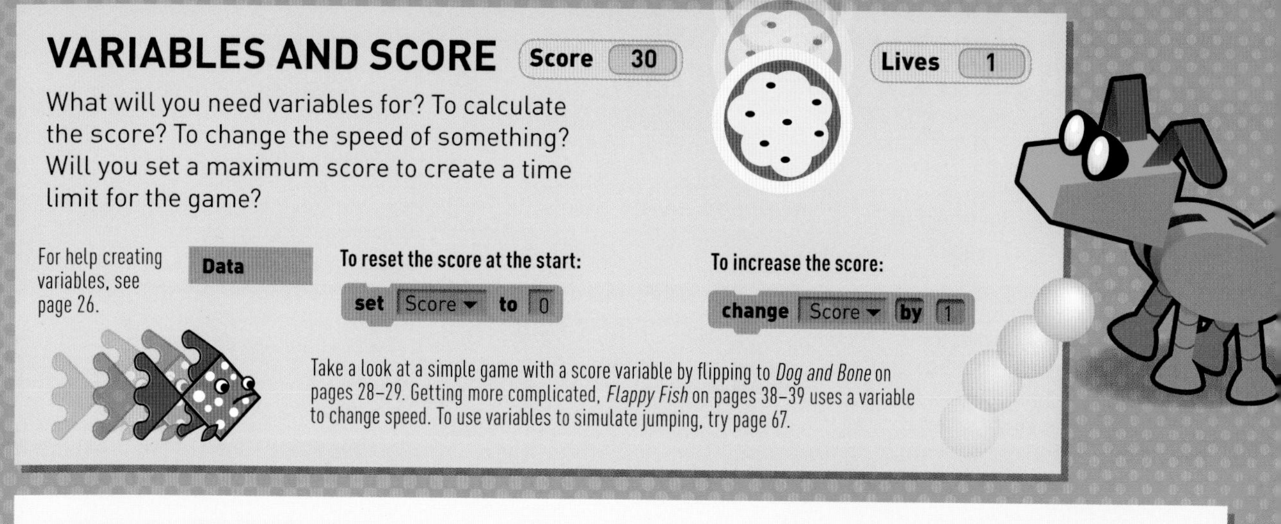

VARIABLES AND SCORE

What will you need variables for? To calculate the score? To change the speed of something? Will you set a maximum score to create a time limit for the game?

For help creating variables, see page 26.

Data

To reset the score at the start:

```
set Score to 0
```

To increase the score:

```
change Score by 1
```

Take a look at a simple game with a score variable by flipping to *Dog and Bone* on pages 28–29. Getting more complicated, *Flappy Fish* on pages 38–39 uses a variable to change speed. To use variables to simulate jumping, try page 67.

SOUND EFFECTS AND ANIMATION

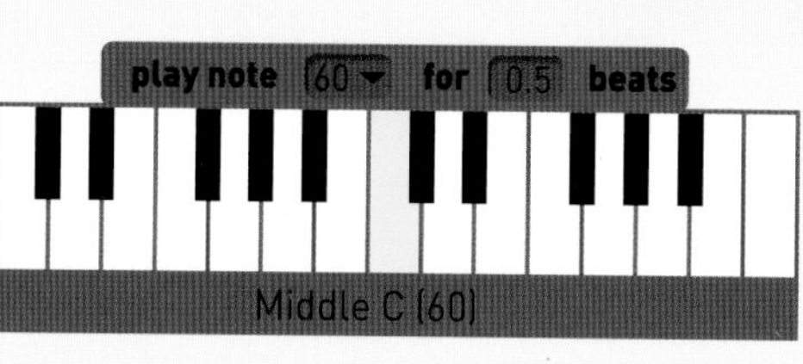

Will you add sound effects? Will these effects be a sound file that is played when something happens, or a tune at the start of the game? Will you use variables to make the sound pitch change as the speed or score goes up?

To play a sound when a key is pressed:

To play a sound when two sprites collide:

```
if touching Cat2 ? then
    play sound meow2 until done
```

To play a short tune:

```
set instrument to 18
play note 60 for 0.5 beats
play note 64 for 0.5 beats
play note 67 for 0.5 beats
play note 72 for 0.5 beats
```

Animations can bring your games to life. Make your sprites look as if they are moving by making wheels turn or wings flap.

If you want to use a sprite from the library with ready-made animations, look for one that has more than one costume. See *Dog and Bone* on pages 28–29.

Dog2
Costumes: 3

To draw your own animated sprite, turn to page 27. There is also a tip on how to add animations to a library sprite on pages 40–41, steps 3–4.

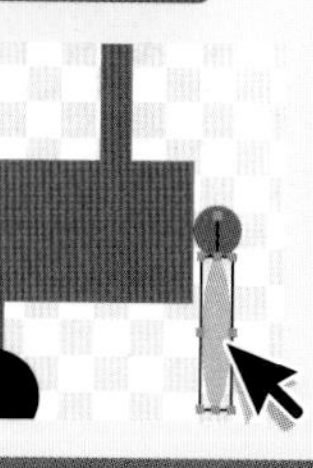

FINALLY . . . TEST AND TEST AGAIN

Don't try to code your whole game straight from start to end. Start by making short programs to test out different parts. For example, create a piece of code that makes your player move around. Experiment with it before you add other parts to the game.

Once you're happy with the basics, you can add details like animations or adjust the scoring system.

Ask other people to try out your game. Does it need instructions? Is it too hard or too easy? Keep experimenting, and don't be afraid to start again.

GLOSSARY

Animation – A series of pictures that are shown one after the other to give the illusion of movement (for example, that a sprite is walking).

Clone – One or more copies of a Scratch sprite. Clones are used to create multiple objects quickly.

Code – A series of instructions or commands.

Code group – The set of Scratch code blocks that control and access variables.

Command – A word or code block that tells the computer what to do.

Coordinates – The position of an object determined by its x (center to right) and y (center to top) values.

Degree – The unit measuring the angle that an object turns.

Drawing Area – The part of the right-hand side of the Scratch screen that is used to draw sprites and backgrounds.

Duplicate – A simple way to create a copy of a sprite in Scratch.

Events group – The set of Scratch code blocks that are triggered when particular events happen, such as a key being pressed.

Function – A sequence of code blocks created to do something, such as move a sprite in a particular way, every time the function is run or "called."

If then – A common form of selection in coding, where command(s) are run if something is true.

Input – An action (like pressing a key) that tells a program to do something.

Language – A system of commands (in the form of blocks, words, or numbers) that tell a computer how to do things.

Loop – A sequence of code blocks repeated a number of times.

Operators group – The set of Scratch code blocks that deals with calculations and comparing values.

Physics engine – A set of commands that simulate the way a real object behaves, for example the way a ball bounces.

Program – The set of commands that tell a computer how to do something such as play a game.

Scratch – A computer language that uses blocks of code to make a program.

Scripts Area – The right-hand side of the Scratch screen where code blocks are dragged to create programs.

Sensing group – The set of Scratch code blocks that detect when specific keys are pressed or where the mouse is.

Speed – How fast an object moves forward. In Scratch, we use negative speed values to move objects backward.

Sprite – An object that moves around the screen.

Sprites Pane – Part of the lower left of the Scratch screen where you select a sprite to add code to or change its appearance.

Stage – The area at the top left of the Scratch screen where you can watch your sprites move about.

Variable – A value or piece of information stored by a computer program. In computer games, a variable is commonly used to store the score.

INDEX